THE SEMIREGULAR POLYTOPES OF THE HYPERSPACES.

THE SEMIREGULAR POLYTOPES OF THE HYPERSPACES.

PROEFSCHRIFT

TER VERKRIJGING VAN DEN GRAAD VAN

Doctor in de Wis- en Natuurkunde,

AAN DE RIJKS-UNIVERSITEIT TE GRONINGEN,

OP GEZAG VAN DEN RECTOR MAGNIFICUS

DR. G. C. NIJHOFF,

HOOGLEERAAR IN DE FACULTEIT DER GENEESKUNDE,

TEGEN DE BEDENKINGEN VAN DE FACULTEIT IN HET OPENBAAR
TE VERDEDIGEN

op Maandag 13 Mei 1912, des namiddags te 3½ uur,

DOOR

EMANUEL LODEWIJK ELTE,

GEBOREN TE AMSTERDAM.

GEBROEDERS HOITSEMA. — GRONINGEN.

AAN DE NAGEDACHTENIS MIJNER MOEDER.

AAN MIJN VADER.

AAN MIJN AANSTAANDE VROUW.

Bij het voltooien van dit proefschrift is het mij een behoefte, aan de hoogleeraren en oud-hoogleeraren der Amsterdamsche Universiteit voor het onderwijs, dat ik van hen ontving, mijn dank te betuigen.

U, Hooggeleerde KORTEWEG, *dank ik voor de wijze waarop Gij mij, bij het ondernemen van dit proefschrift, gesteund en aangemoedigd hebt.*

Hooggeleerde SCHOUTE, *Hooggeschatte Promotor! De belangstelling, die ik van U mocht ondervinden zoowel als de hulp, die Gij mij bij de bewerking van het proefschrift verleende, stemmen mij tot innige dankbaarheid.*

CONTENTS.

CHAPTER I.

DEGREE OF REGULARITY OF THREEDIMENSIONAL POLYHEDRA.

rtex, edge
d face.

§ 1. In the present essay the terms "vertex", "edge" and "face" of a polyhedron have two different meanings.

In the first place they will appear in their usual meaning of points, lines and planes which bound a polyhedron.

In the second place the term "vertex" indicates the polyhedral angle at the vertex (in the usual meaning); the term "edge" includes two things: 1^0. the edge considered as a segment of a line and 2^0. the dihedral angle between the faces which pass through the edge (in the usual meaning); the term "face" indicates a polygon. To a vertex corresponds a spherical polygon on the surface of a sphere described from the vertex as centre. A dihedral angle may be represented by an arc of a circle. Hence "vertex" is a portion of a twodimensional spherical space; "edge" includes a portion of a spherical and a portion of a linear onedimensional space; and "face" is a portion of a linear twodimensional space.

Yet, the twofold meaning of these terms will not give rise to ambiguities. It is obvious indeed that in the sentence "the polyhedron has 18 edges" the word "edge" has its usual meaning, whilst the statement "the polyhedron has equal edges" means that the edges are equally long and that the dihedral angles are equal.

Regular polyhedra.

§ 2. Instead of the common definition we give the following: A polyhedron is regular when its vertices, edges and faces are equal.

It is obvious that this definition includes the five known regular polyhedra. On the other hand nothing may be left out. By leaving out "faces" the definition would include two polyhedra whose vertices are the midpoints of the edges of a cube or of a regular dodecahedron and by leaving out "vertices" their reciprocal polars. By omitting "edges" the definition would include a tetrahedron whose net may be constructed by joining the midpoints of the sides of a scalene triangle.

Henceforth we will represent the regular polyhedra by the initials T, C, O, D and I.

Semiregular polyhedra. Discussion of the number.

§ 3. There are two kinds of semiregular polyhedra, which are generally defined as follows:

A semiregular polyhedron of the first kind has equal (or symmetrical) vertices and regular faces.

A semiregular polyhedron of the second kind has equal faces and regular vertices.

We take the additions "of the first kind" and "of the second kind" from CATALAN [1]).

Those of the first kind are known by the name of "Archimedian".

We will reproduce here the outlines of the theory of these polyhedra. The number of vertices, edges and faces of a polyhedron will be represented by the initials e, k and f of their german equivalents "Ecke" "Kante" and "Flach".

In order to determine the Archimedian polyhedra let us suppose that among the bounding polygons there are f_n

---

1) E. CATALAN, Mémoire sur la théorie des polyèdres. *Journal de l'Ecole Polytechnique*, cahier 47.

of n sides and that these polygons meet to the number of p_n at a vertex of the polyhedron. Then

$$nf_n = p_n e = 2k \quad . \quad . \quad . \quad . \quad . \quad . \quad . \quad (1)$$

whence, by EULER's theorem $(e - k + f = 2)$,

$$e + \Sigma f_n = \tfrac{1}{2} \Sigma n f_n + 2 \quad . \quad . \quad . \quad . \quad . \quad . \quad (2)$$

the summation Σ extending over the number of kinds of bounding polygons. From (2) results, after eliminating f_n by means of (1):

$$e = \frac{4}{2 \Sigma \frac{p_n}{n} + 2 - \Sigma p_n} \quad . \quad . \quad . \quad . \quad . \quad . \quad . \quad (3)$$

This equation must be satisfied by integer values of e, p and n. Now the following remarks[1]) enable to simplify the discussion:

1⁰. The number of kinds of bounding polygons is not less than 2 and not more than 3. For in the case of one kind the polyhedron is regular. In the case of 4 kinds the smallest possible sum of plane angles at a vertex is:

$$60^\circ + 90^\circ + 108^\circ + 120^\circ$$

i. e. more than 360°.

2⁰. No more than 5 edges meet at a vertex. For the smallest sum of plane angles at a vertex, in the case of 6 edges, is

$$5 \times 60^\circ + 90^\circ$$

which is to be rejected for the same reason.

From the latter remark we derive these limits for Σp_n:

$$2 < \Sigma p_n < 6.$$

For the complete discussion we refer to the just mentioned memoir of CATALAN. The result is reproduced in the following list where each polyhedron has a symbol and a

---

1) Dr. P. H. SCHOUTE, Mehrdimensionale Geometrie, II, page 188.

notation. For instance, (12, 18, 8; $1p_3 + 2p_6$) represents a polyhedron bounded by 12 vertices, 18 edges and 8 faces, whilst at a vertex meet one triangle and two hexagons. The notations will be explained in the next art.

No.	Notation.	Symbol.	
1	tT	12, 18, 8;	$1p_3 + 2p_6$
2	tC	24, 36, 14;	$1p_3 + 2p_8$
3	tO	24, 36, 14;	$1p_4 + 2p_6$
4	tD	60, 90, 32;	$1p_3 + 2p_{10}$
5	tI	60, 90, 32;	$1p_5 + 2p_6$
6	CO	12, 24, 14;	$2p_3 + 2p_4$
7	ID	30, 60, 32;	$2p_3 + 2p_5$
8	RCO	24, 48, 26;	$1p_3 + 3p_4$
9	RID	60, 120, 62;	$1p_3 + 2p_4 + 1p_5$
10	tCO	48, 72, 26;	$1p_4 + 1p_6 + 1p_8$
11	tID	120, 180, 62;	$1p_4 + 1p_6 + 1p_{10}$
12	CS	24, 60, 38;	$1p_4 + 4p_3$
13	DS	60, 150, 92;	$1p_5 + 4p_3$
14	P_n	$2n$, $3n$, $n + 2$;	$1p_n + 2p_4$
15	AP_n	$2n$, $4n$, $2n + 2$;	$1p + 3p_3$

Construction of the semi-regular polyhedra of the first kind.

§ 4. We will now explain how the Archimedian polyhedra may be constructed.

The Nos. 1—5 may be derived from the regular polyhedra by means of regular truncation at the vertices, so that the faces are transformed into regular polygons of double the number of sides. This operation is indicated by the *t* before the letter representing the polyhedron to be truncated.

No. 6 may be derived from C by truncation at the vertices as far as the midpoints of the edges; or by the same operation from O. This twofold origin is indicated by CO. KEPLER[1]) calls it Cuboctaëdron.

In the same way No. 7 may be derived from D or I. KEPLER[1]) calls it Icosidodecaëdron. We will represent it by ID.

No. 8 may be derived from C by drawing in the bounding squares equal concentric squares having their sides parallel to the edges of C. Then the 24 vertices of the squares are the vertices of 8 equilateral triangles near the vertices of C and 12 rectangles parallel to the edges of C. Now we are able, by making the squares small enough, to produce rectangles with the longer side perpendicular to the corresponding edge of C; and by making them large enough to produce rectangles with the longer side parallel to that edge. So there must be an intermediate position in which the rectangles are squares.

The notation RCO is an abbreviation of Rhombicuboctaëdron. This is a combination of CO and a polyhedron limited by 12 lozenges (rhombi) which can be obtained by means of the planes through the edges of a C normal to the lines joining the midpoints of the edges to the centre of C. This (14, 24, 12) is reciprocal polar of No. 6.

The analogous operation on D leads to No. 9 (RID = Rhombicosidodecaëdron).

No. 10 may be derived from C in a similar way as No. 8 but now by placing in the squares of C equal concentric octagons having their alternate sides parallel to the edges of C. In this case the polygons at the vertices of C are hexagons. The notation tCO is an abbreviation of Kepler's Truncum Cuboctaëdron. Yet we must draw the attention to the fact that it is impossible to derive tCO from CO by truncation, as the *t* might suggest. What may be derived in this way from CO, is a polyhedron which is *isomorph* to tCO.

---

1) KEPLER, *Harmonices Mundi*, liber II, prop. XXVIII.

The analogous operation on D leads to No. 11 (tID = Truncum Icosidodecaëdron).

In order to construct No. 12 we draw squares in the faces of a C as in the case of RCO. The side of such a square may be represented by l. Then we turn these squares in their respective planes about their centre through an angle α and in the same direction for a spectator looking from the centre of C. Then again the 24 vertices of the squares are the vertices of 8 equilateral triangles near the vertices of C. But two sides near an edge of C, such as EH and BC of fig. 1 are not situated in the same plane. So by drawing the 12 lines BH, KG, CN etc. we get two triangles per edge of C. Now if we take l and α at random these 24 equal triangles are scalene. But we may dispose of l and α so as to make BH = HC and HC = CB.

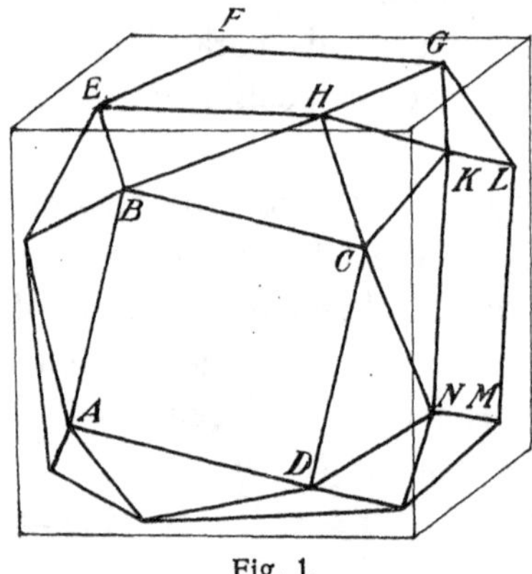

Fig. 1.

CS is an abbreviation of Kepler's *Cubus Simus*, which name characterizes the appearance of this polyhedron. It means literally "flat cube". In fact, the polyhedron is very much like a cube whose vertices and edges are worn out.

The analogous operation on D leads to No. 13 (DS = Dodecaëdron Simum).

No. 14 includes an infinite number of polyhedra, viz. regular n-angular prisms whose lateral faces are squares.

No. 15 includes an infinite number of polyhedra, which are called *antiprisms*. An AP_n may be derived from an n-angular regular prism by turning one of the bases through an angle of $\frac{360^\circ}{2n}$ about the axis of the prism. Then by joining each vertex to the two nearest vertices of the opposite base we get $2n$ isoceles triangles. Now by giving the altitude of the prism a proper value we may get equilateral triangles.

The two latter Nos. include as special cases:

$$P_4 = C$$
$$AP_3 = O.$$

Thus, P_n and AP_n excepted, any Archimedian polyhedron is derivable from a regular one. The formulae giving the edges of the former in terms of those of the latter and other metrical relations may be found in the textbook of BRÜCKNER [1]). They are of no interest for our purpose. What will be of importance for our present investigations is the computation of the dihedral and solid angles.

Dihedral angles, solid angles. § 5. For that purpose we state the following theorems:

I. A semiregular polyhedron of the first kind admits a circumscribed sphere.

II. The dihedral angles between equal couples of faces are equal.

Thus in tT there are two kinds of angles: those between a triangle and a hexagon and those between two hexagons. In CO there is only one kind of dihedral angle.

Now, let an Archimedian polyhedron be inscribed in a sphere of unit radius. Then by joining the vertices by portions of great circles, subtended by edges of the polyhedron, the surface of the sphere is divided into regular spherical polygons of 2 or 3 kinds, meeting in a similar way at the vertices. Let the side of the polygons be

---

[1]) Dr. MAX BRÜCKNER, *Vielecke und Vielflache*, p. 132—140. This book gives excellent diagrams.

represented by y, the angle of a regular polygon of n sides by x_n, then by a formula of spherical trigonometry

$$\cos \tfrac{1}{2}y = \frac{\cos \dfrac{\pi}{n}}{\sin \tfrac{1}{2}x_n} \quad . \quad . \quad . \quad . \quad . \quad . \quad . \quad (4)$$

We have as many of these equations as there are kinds of polygons. Besides we know that the sum of the angles at a vertex is 2π, whence

$$\Sigma p_n x_n = 2\pi, \quad . \quad . \quad . \quad . \quad . \quad . \quad . \quad . \quad (5)$$

p_n representing the number of polygons of n sides at a vertex. By the equations (4) and (5) we are able to determine y and x_n.

Let R_n be the radius of the circumscribing circle of a polygon of n sides, then

$$\sin R_n = \frac{\sin \tfrac{1}{2}y}{\sin \dfrac{\pi}{n}} \quad . \quad . \quad . \quad . \quad . \quad . \quad . \quad . \quad (6)$$

When AB represents the common edge of the faces f_m and f_n of m and n sides respectively, then, after dropping perpendiculars from the centre O of the polyhedron which meet the faces in M and N and the edge AB in C, the angle MCN between f_m and f_n is equal to $\angle MCO + \angle NCO$ whose cosines are

$$\cos MCO = \frac{MC}{OC}, \quad \cos NCO = \frac{NC}{OC} \cdot$$

Now

$$OC = \cos \tfrac{1}{2}y,$$

$$MC = MA \cos \frac{\pi}{m} = \sin R_n \cos \frac{\pi}{m},$$

and by form. (6)

$$MC = \sin \tfrac{1}{2}y \cot \frac{\pi}{m} \cdot$$

Hence

$$\cos \text{MCO} = \frac{\text{tg} \frac{1}{2} y}{\text{tang} \frac{\pi}{m}}, \quad \cos \text{NCO} = \frac{\text{tang} \frac{1}{2} y}{\text{tang} \frac{\pi}{n}},$$

$$\angle \text{MCN} = \cos^{-1} \frac{\text{tang} \frac{1}{2} y}{\text{tang} \frac{\pi}{m}} + \cos^{-1} \frac{\text{tang} \frac{1}{2} y}{\text{tang} \frac{\pi}{n}} \quad . \quad . \quad (7)$$

Thus, in order to calculate the angles, we have to eliminate the x_n from the equations (4) and (5), the n and p being given by the symbol of the polyhedron. Then after calculating y the formulae (7) give the required angles.

The following table gives the dihedral angles and solid angles of the semiregular (P_n and AP_n up to $n = 10$) and regular polyhedra. For the polyhedra bounded by more than one kind of polygons, the numbers between ( ) denote the number of sides of the polygons which include the dihedral angle.

Semiregular polyhedra of the second kind.

§ 6. By constructing the planes polar to the vertices of a semiregular polyhedron of the first kind we enclose a polyhedron having equal faces and regular vertices, thus a semiregular polyhedron of the second kind. This statement implies a method of construction.

A semiregular polyhedron of the second kind will be represented by the accented notation of the corresponding semiregular polyhedron of the first kind.

Degree of regularity.

§ 7. We say that a regular polyhedron shows 3 *characteristics of regularity* viz. equality of vertices, of edges and of faces. The second characteristic includes two equalities which may appear separately. So e. g. tT has equally long edges, (tT)′ equal dihedral angles. Now we say that these polyhedra have *half the second characteristic*. Either of both polyhedra shows half the number of characteristics

	Dihedral angles.			Solid angles.
T	70° 31′ 43″, 624			31° 35′ 10″, 872
C	90°			90°
O	109° 28′ 16″, 376			77° 53′ 5″, 604
D	116° 33′ 54″, 184			169° 41′ 42″, 552
I	138° 11′ 22″, 866			150° 56′ 54″, 300
tT	(6,6) = 70° 31′ 43″, 624	(6,3) = 109° 28′ 16″, 376		109° 28′ 16″, 376
tC	(8,8) = 90°	(8,3) = 125° 15′ 51″, 812		160° 31′ 43″, 624
tO	(6,6) = 109° 28′ 16″, 376	(6,4) = 125° 15′ 51″, 812		180°
tD	(10,10) = 116° 33′ 54″, 184	(10,3) = 142° 37′ 21″, 475		221° 48′ 37″, 134
tI	(6,6) = 138° 11′ 22″, 866	(6,5) = 142° 37′ 21″, 475		243° 26′ 5″, 816
CO	125° 15′ 51″, 812			141° 3′ 27″, 248
ID	142° 37′ 21″, 475			210° 29′ 25″, 900
RCO	(4,4) = 135°	(4,3) = 144° 44′ 8″, 188		199° 28′ 16″, 376
RID	(4,5) = 148° 16′ 57″, 092	(4,3) = 159° 5′ 41″, 433		254° 45′ 17″, 050
tCO	(6,8) = 125° 15′ 51″, 812	(4,8) = 135°	(4,6) = 144° 44′ 8″, 188	225°
tID	(10,6) = 142° 37′ 21″, 475	(10,4) = 148° 16′ 57″, 092	(4,6) = 159° 5′ 41″, 433	270°
CS	(4,3) = 142° 59′ 0″, 093	(3,3) = 153° 14′ 4″, 340		145° 40′ 13″, 206
DS	(5,3) = 152° 55′ 53″, 600	(3,3) = 164° 10′ 31″, 322		198° 23′ 21″, 166
P_3	(4,4) = 60°	(3,4) = 90°		60°
P_4	(4,4) = 90°			90°
P_5	(4,4) = 108°	(5,4) = 90°		108°
P_6	(4,4) = 120°	(6,4) = 90°		120°
P_8	(4,4) = 135°	(8,4) = 90°		135°
P_{10}	(4,4) = 144°	(10,4) = 90°		144°
AP_3		109° 28′ 16″, 376		77° 53′ 5″, 576
AP_4	(4,3) = 103° 50′ 11″, 350	(3,3) = 127° 33′ 5″, 760		94° 43′ 40″, 180
AP_5	(5,3) = 100° 48′ 44″, 341	(3,3) = 138° 11′ 22″, 866		118° 0′ 14″, 414
AP_6	(6,3) = 98° 54′ 57″, 944	(3,3) = 145° 13′ 18″, 986		128° 16′ 33″, 960
AP_8	(8,3) = 96° 35′ 40″, 284	(3,3) = 153° 57′ 47″, 572		141° 6′ 49″, 712
AP_{10}	(10,3) = 95° 14′ 44″, 915	(3,3) = 159° 11′ 9″, 678		148° 51′ 55″, 186

of a regular one and exactly those characteristics which are wanting in the other as is shown in the subjoined sketch.

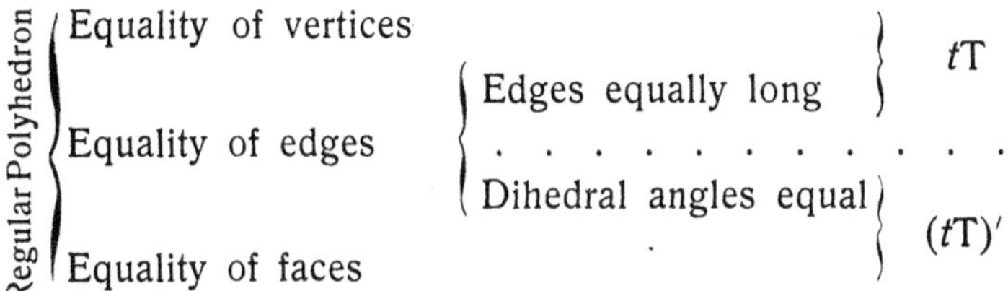

Now we state the following definition: *The degree of regularity of a polyhedron is a fraction whose denominator is* 3 *and whose numerator is the number of characteristics of regularity of the polyhedron.* Whether the characteristics begin at „vertex'' or at "face" will be indicated by the additions "of the first kind'' and "of the second kind.''

By this definition a regular prism whose lateral faces differ from squares has a degree of regularity of $\frac{1}{3}$ and is of the first kind.

The semiregular polyhedra have the degree $\frac{1\frac{1}{2}}{3} = \frac{1}{2}$, except CO, ID, (CO)′ and (ID)′, which show the complete second characteristic and consequently have the degree $\frac{2}{3}$.

The tetrahedron mentioned in art. 2 shows two complete characteristics viz. equality of vertices and equality of faces. Yet we will not call it $\frac{2}{3}$ regular, as the series of characteristics is interrupted by the lack of the second characteristic. So we add to our definition that *by the expression "number of characteristics" only immediately consecutive characteristics will be meant.*

The just mentioned tetrahedron will be considered of the first kind as having only equal vertices and of the second kind as having only equal faces; hence its degree of regularity is $\frac{1}{3}$ of the first or second kind. In moredimensional spaces instances of interrupted regularity are more common.

CHAPTER II.

FOURDIMENSIONAL SEMIREGULAR POLYTOPES OF THE FIRST KIND. THE FIVE ALLREADY KNOWN ONES.

Vertex, edge, face and space. § 8. The number of vertices, edges, faces and (three-dimensional) spaces which bound a polytope in a fourdimensional space S_4 will be represented by E, K, F and R, R being the intial of the german "Raum".

As in the preceding chapter the terms "vertex" "edge" "face" and "space" have two meanings. Thus, besides their usual meaning

"vertex" denotes a portion of a threedimensional spherical space,
„edge" „ „ „ „ „ onedimensional linear „ ,
and „ „ „ „ two „ spherical „ ,
"face" denotes „ „ „ „ „ „ linear „ ,
and „ „ „ „ one „ spherical „ ,
and "space" „ „ „ „ three „ linear „ ,

Regular cells. § 9. There are 6 regular cells in S_4 namely [1]):

$$C_5 \quad (5, 10, 10, 5; 3, 4)_T$$
$$C_{16} \quad (8, 24, 32, 16; 4, 8)_T$$
$$C_8 \quad (16, 32, 24, 8; 3, 4)_C$$
$$C_{24} \quad (24, 96, 96, 96; 3, 6)_O$$
$$C_{600} \quad (120, 720, 1200, 600; 5, 20)_T$$
$$C_{120} \quad (600, 1200, 720, 120; 3, 4)_D$$

---

1) A detailed description of the regular cells may be found in Dr. P. H. SCHOUTE, Mehrdimensionale Geometrie II, p. 196—243.

Taking e. g. C_{16}, the symbol is to be read as follows: C_{16} is bounded by 8 vertices, 24 edges, 32 faces and 16 spaces, whilst the latter meet to the number of 4 at an edge and to the number of 8 at a vertex. The bounding polyhedra are T.

Degree of regularity. Vertex polyhedron. Edge polygon.

§ 10. The following definition is an extension of that in art. 7. *The degree of regularity of a fourdimensional polytope is a fraction whose denominator is 4 and whose numerator is the number of consecutive characteristics of regularity.* Whether the series of characteristics begins at "vertex" or at "space" will be indicated by the addition "of the first kind" and "of the second kind".

Here the second and third characteristics are divisible.

For polytopes of degree $\frac{1}{2}$ and more we introduce the *vertex polyhedron* and the *edge polygon:*

By a *vertex polyhedron of a polytope* P we understand *the polyhedron of which the endpoints of the edges issuing from a vertex of P are the vertices.*

By an *edge polygon of P* we understand *the polygon of which the endpoints of the edges that issue from a vertex of the vertex polyhedron of P are the vertices.*

Thus the vertex polyhedron of C_5, C_8, C_{120} is T, that of C_{16} is O, that of C_{24} is C and that of C_{600} is I; the edge polygons are p_3, p_4 and p_5 respectively.

Truncation half way up the edges of the regular cells.

§ 11. The aim of the present investigation is to determine the polytopes in R_4 the degree of regularity of which is at least $\frac{1}{2}$. We will begin by examining more closely five polytopes which were described by Mrs. A. Boole Stott and prof. P. H. Schoute in a paper published by the Amsterdam Academy [1]). From this paper we take

---

[1]) Proceedings Royal Acad. Amsterdam, X p. 499.

the following table where P represents the number of spaces through an edge, and Q that through a vertex.

Derived from	E	K	T	R	P	Q
C_5	10	30	30	10	3	5
C_8	32	96	88	24	3	5
C_{24}	96	288	240	48	3	5
C_{600}	720	3600	3600	720	3	7
C_{120}	1200	3600	3120	720	3	5

Before proceeding to investigate these polytopes separately we remark that there are two kinds of bounding polyhedra viz. truncating and truncated ones; the former to the number of vertices of the corresponding regular cell, the latter to the number of spaces of that cell. The latter are the result of the truncation half way up the edges of a regular polyhedron, being in the order of the above table

O, CO, CO, O, ID.

The truncating polyhedron is similar to the vertex polyhedron of the regular cell, hence

T, T, C, I, T.

Now applying these observations to the case of C_{16}, we find that both truncating and truncated polyhedron are O_8. Indeed the operation on C_{16} leads to C_{24}. Therefore C_{16} is wanting in the table.

(10, 30, 30, 10). § 12. Let E_1, E_2, E_3, E_4 and E_5 represent the vertices of a C_5 and E_{12}, E_{13} etc. the midpoints of the edges; then for the polytope whose vertices are these midpoints we find $E = (5)_2 = 10$.

An edge is situated in a face of C_5 and thus joins two vertices whose indices have one figure in common. Hence E_{12} is joined by edges to E_{13}, E_{14}, E_{15}, E_{23}, E_{24} and E_{25}.

The edge passing through E_{12} and E_{13} will be represented by $K_{\overset{+}{1}23}$, the sign $+$ upon 1 indicating that 1 appears in the indices of both endpoints of the edge. From this notation we infer that $K = 3\,(5)_3 = 30$.

A face is either part of a face of C_5 (e. g. triangle $E_{12}\,E_{13}\,E_{23}$) or truncates a T of C_5 (e. g. $E_{12}\,E_{13}\,E_{14}$). The former is represented by $F_{\overset{-}{4}\overset{-}{5}}$ (the signs — indicating that 4 and 5 do *not* appear in the indices of the vertices of the triangle). Their number is $(5)_2 = 10$. The latter is represented by $F_{\overset{+}{1}\overset{-}{5}}$. Their number is $2 \times (5)_2 = 20$. Hence $F = 30$.

The truncating polyhedron (T) at E_1 will be represented by $T_{\overset{+}{1}}$, the truncated (O) in $E_1\,E_2\,E_3\,E_4$ by $O_{\overset{-}{5}}$; $R = 10$.

$O_{\overset{-}{1}}$ is bounded by the faces

$$F_{\overset{-}{1}\overset{-}{2}},\quad F_{\overset{-}{1}\overset{-}{3}},\quad F_{\overset{-}{1}\overset{-}{4}},\quad F_{\overset{-}{1}\overset{-}{5}}$$
$$F_{\overset{-}{1}\overset{+}{2}},\quad F_{\overset{-}{1}\overset{+}{3}},\quad F_{\overset{-}{1}\overset{+}{4}},\quad F_{\overset{-}{1}\overset{+}{5}}.$$

Any two faces on the same line have one and only one vertex in common (so e. g. $F_{\overset{-}{1}\overset{-}{3}}$ and $F_{\overset{-}{1}\overset{-}{5}}$ have E_{24}, $F_{\overset{-}{1}\overset{+}{3}}$ and $F_{\overset{-}{1}\overset{+}{5}}$ have E_{35} in common), any face has an edge in common with the three non-corresponding faces on the other line (so e. g. $F_{\overset{-}{1}\overset{+}{3}}$ has in common with $F_{\overset{-}{1}\overset{+}{2}}$, $F_{\overset{-}{1}\overset{+}{4}}$ and $F_{\overset{-}{1}\overset{+}{5}}$ the edges $K_{\overset{+}{2}45}$, $K_{2\overset{+}{4}5}$ and $K_{24\overset{+}{5}}$ respectively). Hence the faces on the same line represent a set of alternate faces of O. Now the differently notated faces are of different kind. A face of the first line $F_{\overset{-}{1}\overset{-}{2}}$ belongs to an other octahedron $O_{\overset{-}{2}}$. A face of the second line $F_{\overset{-}{1}\overset{+}{2}}$ belongs to a tetrahedron $T_{\overset{+}{2}}$. So *the former* is the boundary of two *equal polyhedra* and will be called a *homogeneous face*, the *latter* of two *different polyhedra* and will be called a *heterogeneous face*.

An edge $K_{\overset{+}{1}23}$ belongs to $T_{\overset{+}{1}}$, $O_{\overset{-}{4}}$ and $O_{\overset{-}{5}}$. The intersection of an S_8, perpendicular to the edge, and these three polyhedra is an isosceles trihedral angle as two sides are 109° 28′ 16″, 4 (being the dihedral angle of O) and the third 70° 31′ 43″, 6 (ditto of T). (The edge opposite to the latter side corresponds to a homogeneous face; the two remaining ones to heterogeneous faces). Hence we call the edge of the polytope *isosceles*.

Through a vertex E_{12} pass $T_{\substack{+\\1}}$, $T_{\substack{+\\2}}$, $O_{\substack{-\\3}}$, $O_{\substack{-\\4}}$ and $O_{\substack{-\\5}}$, moreover the homogeneous faces $F_{\substack{-\,-\\3\,4}}$, $F_{\substack{-\,-\\3\,5}}$, $F_{\substack{-\,-\\4\,5}}$ and the heterogeneous ones $F_{\substack{-\,+\\3\,1}}$, $F_{\substack{-\,+\\4\,1}}$, $F_{\substack{-\,+\\5\,1}}$, $F_{\substack{-\,+\\3\,2}}$, $F_{\substack{-\,+\\4\,2}}$ and $F_{\substack{-\,+\\5\,2}}$. Hence the spherical polyhedron corresponding to a vertex is bounded by 2 regular triangles and 3 regular tetragons; by 9 equally long edges — of which 3 are homogeneous and 6 heterogeneous — whilst to the 6 edges that issue from E_{12} correspond 6 equal isosceles vertices. Now if we extend the rule for determining the degree of regularity of a polyhedron to a spherical one, our polyhedron has the degree $\frac{1}{2}$. Hence we call a *vertex* of the polytope *regular of degree* $\frac{1}{2}$.

This result may be obtained more easily by considering the vertex polyhedron, which has the same degree of regularity as the spherical polyhedron corresponding to a vertex. It is in our case a P_8.

In the same way, from the fact that the edge polygon is an isosceles triangle we infer that the edge of the polytope is isosceles.

The degree of regularity of the polytope is $\frac{5}{8}$ of the first kind. Indeed it shows $2\frac{1}{2}$ characteristics of regularity.

32, 96, 88, 24). § 13. In order to investigate the result of the truncation of C_8 we introduce a set of notations closely connected with the rectangular system of axes whose origin is the centre of C_8 and whose axes pass through the centres of the cubes. With respect to that system the coordinates of the vertices are

$$(\pm \tfrac{1}{2}, \pm \tfrac{1}{2}, \pm \tfrac{1}{2}, \pm \tfrac{1}{2}),$$

the length of an edge taken as unit. This symbol includes all the possible combinations of signs to the number of $2^4 = 16$. Now we will represent a vertex whose coordinates are e. g. $(+\tfrac{1}{2}, -\tfrac{1}{2}, +\tfrac{1}{2}, +\tfrac{1}{2})$ by E_{+-++}.

An edge of C_8 passes through two vertices whose indices differ in one sign only. For an edge joining E_{+-++} to E_{--++} we introduce the symbol K_{0-++}. A bounding square is represented by F_{0-0+}, a cube by R_{0-00}.

After truncating C_8 we represent a vertex of the resulting polytope by the same index as the corresponding edge of C_8, but that index in connection with E. Thus E_{0-++} is the midpoint of K_{0-++}. So $E = 32$.

An edge truncates a square of C_8 at a vertex. The edge truncating F_{0-0+} at E_{+-++} will be represented by $K_{(+)-(+)+}$. This edge joins E_{0-++} to E_{+-0+}.

Through E_{0-++} pass the following edges:

$K_{(+)-+(+)}$, $K_{(-)-+(+)}$ in F_{0-+0},
$K_{(+)-(+)+}$, $K_{(-)-(+)+}$ in F_{0-0+},
$K_{(+)(-)++}$, $K_{(-)(-)++}$ in F_{00++}. So $K = \dfrac{6 \times 32}{2} = 96.$

There are two kinds of faces:

1^0. squares to the number of 24 which are parts of the squares of C_8 and which will be represented by the *same* notations.

2^0. triangles which truncate the cubes; we represent the triangle which truncates R_{000+} at the vertex E_{+-++} by $F_{(+)(-)(+)+}$.

Their number is $2^4 \times (4)_3 = 64$. Hence $F = 64 + 24 = 88$.

A cube of C_8 e. g. R_{+000} is transformed into CO, which we will denote by the same index: $(CO)_{+00}$.

A truncating T at the vertex E_{+-++} will be represented by T_{+-++}. So $R = 8 + 16 = 24$.

A square F_{++00} bounds two CO viz.: $(CO)_{+000}$ and $(CO)_{0+00}$ and is consequently homogeneous.

A triangle $F_{+(+)(-)(+)}$ belongs to $(CO)_{+000}$ and to no other CO. Besides it belongs to T_{++-+}. Hence a triangle is heterogeneous. Thus in this case the faces are completely unequal.

Through an edge $K_{(+)-(+)+}$ pass the square F_{0-0+} and the triangles $F_{(+)(-)(+)+}$ and $F_{(+)-(+)(+)}$, the polyhedra $(CO)_{000+}$, $(CO)_{0-0+}$ and T_{+-++}.

We stated higher up that 6 edges issue from one vertex. Hence the vertex polyhedron has 6 vertices. From what we said about the edge of the polytope we infer that through a vertex of the vertex polyhedron pass two rectangles with sides equal to 1 and $\sqrt{2}$ and one triangle whose side is 1 in terms of the edge of the polytope. Besides from the notation E_{0-++} we infer that through a vertex of the polytope pass

$$(CO)_{000+},\ (CO)_{00+0},\ (CO)_{0-00},$$
$$T_{+-++},\ T_{--++}.$$

Hence the vertex polyhedron is a regular triangular prism. Its degree of regularity is $\frac{1}{3}$.

The edge polygon is again an isosceles triangle. Thus the edge is isosceles.

The degree of regularity of the polytope is $\frac{1}{2}$ of the first kind.

(96, 288, 240, 48). § 14. We will now investigate the polytope derived from C_{24}. We can obtain C_{24} by truncating C_{16} half way up the edges (art. 11).

Henceforth a set of coordinates between ( ) will include all the sets that can be derived from it by means of permutation; a set between [ ] those which can be derived by permutation while to each arrangement must be attributed all the possible combinations of signs. Hence a set of 4 different coordinates none of which is $=0$ represents 24 sets if placed between ( ) and 384 sets if placed between [ ].

The edges, faces and spaces will be represented by the coordinates of their centres.

We can represent the limits of C_{16} by

E	$[4, 0, 0, 0]$	8
K	$[2, 2, 0, 0]$	24
p_3	$[\frac{4}{3}, \frac{4}{3}, \frac{4}{3}, 0]$	32
T	$[1, 1, 1, 1]$	16

Length of edge $= 4\sqrt{2}$.

Now if we truncate C_{16} as far as the midpoints of the edges both the truncated and truncating polyhedra are O. We will call them *quasi-truncated* and *quasi-truncating* respectively.

The quasi-truncated O

$$1, 1, 1, 1$$

is bounded by

E	$(2, 2, 0, 0)$	24
K	$(2, 1, 1, 0)$	96
p_3	$(2, \frac{2}{3}, \frac{2}{3}, \frac{2}{3})$	64
p_3	$(0, \frac{4}{3}, \frac{4}{3}, \frac{4}{3})$	32

The quasi-truncating O which truncates C_{16} at the vertex

$$4, 0, 0, 0$$

is represented by

$$2, 0, 0, 0$$

and bounded by

E	$2, [2, 0, 0]$	6
K	$2, [1, 1, 0]$	12
p_3	$2, [\frac{2}{3}, \frac{2}{3}, \frac{2}{3}]$	8

Hence the limits of C_{24} are

E	$[2, 2, 0, 0]$	24
K	$[2, 1, 1, 0]$	96

$p_3\,[2,\ \tfrac{2}{3},\ \tfrac{2}{3},\ \tfrac{2}{3}]$ 64
$p_3\,[0,\ \tfrac{4}{3},\ \tfrac{4}{3},\ \tfrac{4}{3}]$ 32
O [1, 1, 1, 1] 16
O [2, 0, 0, 0] 8

Length of edge $= 2\sqrt{2}$.

Any of the $p_3\ [2,\ \tfrac{2}{3},\ \tfrac{2}{3},\ \tfrac{2}{3}]$ is situated between a quasi-truncated O and a quasi-truncating one, any of the $p_3\,[0,\ \tfrac{4}{3},\ \tfrac{4}{3},\ \tfrac{4}{3}]$ between two quasi-truncated O.

We will now truncate C_{24} as far as the midpoints of the edges. The quasi-truncated O

1, 1, 1, 1

is transformed into a CO, which is represented by the same notation, and whose limits are

E (2, 1, 1, 0) 12
K $(2,\ 1,\ \tfrac{1}{2},\ \tfrac{1}{2})$ 12
K $(1,\ 0,\ \tfrac{3}{2},\ \tfrac{3}{2})$ 12
$p_4\ (\tfrac{3}{2},\ \tfrac{3}{2},\ \tfrac{1}{2},\ \tfrac{1}{2})$ 4
$p_3\ (2,\ \tfrac{2}{3},\ \tfrac{2}{3},\ \tfrac{2}{3})$ 4
$p_3\ (0,\ \tfrac{4}{3},\ \tfrac{4}{3},\ \tfrac{4}{3})$ 4

The CO

2, 0, 0, 0,

derived from the equally notated quasi-truncating O, is bounded by

E 2, [1, 1, 0] 12
K 2, $[1,\ \tfrac{1}{2},\ \tfrac{1}{2}]$ 24
p_4 2, [1, 0, 0] 6
p_3 2, $[\tfrac{2}{3},\ \tfrac{2}{3},\ \tfrac{2}{3}]$ 8

The C that truncates C_{24} at the vertex

2, 2, 0, 0

is represented by

$\tfrac{3}{2},\ \tfrac{3}{2},\ 0,\ 0$

and bounded by

E	$(2, 1), [1, 0]$	8
K	$(2, 1), [\frac{1}{2}, \frac{1}{2}]$	8
	$\frac{3}{2}, \frac{3}{2}, [1, 0]$	4
p_4	$\frac{3}{2}, \frac{3}{2}, [\frac{1}{2}, \frac{1}{2}]$	4
	$(2, 1), 0, 0$	2

Hence the limits of the polytope are

E	$[2, 1, 1, 0]$	96
K	$[2, 1, \frac{1}{2}, \frac{1}{2}]$	192
	$[\frac{3}{2}, \frac{3}{2}, 1, 0]$	96
p_3	$[2, \frac{2}{3}, \frac{2}{3}, \frac{2}{3}]$	64
	$[\frac{4}{3}, \frac{4}{3}, \frac{4}{3}, 0]$	32
p_4	$[2, 1, 0, 0]$	48
	$[\frac{3}{2}, \frac{3}{2}, \frac{1}{2}, \frac{1}{2}]$	96
C	$[\frac{3}{2}, \frac{3}{2}, 0, 0]$	24
CO	$[1, 1, 1, 1]$	16
	$[2, 0, 0, 0]$	8

Length of edge $= \sqrt{2}$.

We will now determine the degree of regularity. The p_3 are equal. Indeed through the triangles

$p_3\,[2, \frac{2}{3}, \frac{2}{3}, \frac{2}{3}]$ pass CO $[2, 0, 0, 0]$ and CO$[1, 1, 1, 1]$,
$p_3\,[\frac{4}{3}, \frac{4}{3}, \frac{4}{3}, 0]$ „ CO $[1, 1, 1, 1]$ „ CO$[1, 1, 1, -1]$ [1]).
Hence the p_3 are homogeneous.

The p_4 are equal. Indeed through the squares

$p_4\,[\frac{3}{2}, \frac{3}{2}, \frac{1}{2}, \frac{1}{2}]$ pass CO $[1, 1, 1, 1]$ and C $[\frac{3}{2}, \frac{3}{2}, 0, 0]$,
$p_4\,[2, 1, 0, 0]$ „ CO $[2, 0, 0, 0]$ „ C $[\frac{3}{2}, \frac{3}{2}, 0, 0]$.
Hence the p_4 are heterogeneous. So there are two kinds of faces.

The edges are equal. Through
K $[2, 1, \frac{1}{2}, \frac{1}{2}]$ pass CO $[1, 1, 1, 1]$, CO $[2, 0, 0, 0]$ and C $[\frac{3}{2}, \frac{3}{2}, 0, 0]$ and through

---

1) The meaning of [ ] in this and analogous cases is: The statement holds after applying any operation indicated by [ ] on all the symbols that appear in the statement.

K $[\frac{3}{2}, \frac{3}{2}, 1, 0]$ pass CO $[1, 1, 1, 1]$, CO $[1, 1, 1, -1]$ and $[\frac{3}{2}, \frac{3}{2}, 0, 0]$

Hence the edges are isosceles.

The vertices are equal. Through

$$E\,[2, 1, 1, 0]$$

pass

$$CO\,[1, 1, 1, 1],\ CO\,[1, 1, 1, -1],\ CO\,[2, 0, 0, 0]$$
$$C\,[\tfrac{3}{2}, \tfrac{3}{2}, 0, 0],\ C\,[\tfrac{3}{2}, 0, \tfrac{3}{2}, 0]$$

Hence the polytope shows 2 characteristics of regularity. Its degree of regularity is $\frac{1}{2}$.

The vertex polyhedron is a 3-angular prism, the edges of the bases are $= \sqrt{2}$, the lateral edges $= 1$ in terms of the edge of the polytope.

(720, 3600, 3600, 720). § 15. In truncating C_{600} as far as the midpoints of the edges the bounding T are transformed into O, while the truncating polyhedra are I.

We will introduce beforehand the symbol

$$[a, b, c, d]\tfrac{1}{2}$$

where a, b, c and d are coordinates. It includes all the sets of coordinates which are derivable by means of the *even substitutions* and *all the combinations of signs.* The even substitutions of 4 elements a, b, c and d are the following: (bcd), (cda), (dab), (abc), (bdc), (cad), (dba), (acb), $(ab)(cd)$, $(ac)(bd)$, $(ad)(bc)$ and 1.

Here (bcd) represents a cyclic substitution, b being replaced by c, c by d and d by b, whilst (ab) indicates the transposition of the elements a and b, and 1 the identical operation

Hence $[\,]\frac{1}{2}$ applied to four different coordinates of which none is $= 0$ represents 192 sets of coordinates. It is obvious that there is no difference whatever between $[\,]$ and $[\,]\frac{1}{2}$ as soon as at least two coordinates are equal.

In the present investigation we will often refer to a

memoir by Dr. P. H. SCHOUTE[1]) entitled: "Regelmässige Schnitte und Projectionen des Hundertzwanzigzelles und Sechshundertzelles im vierdimensionalen Raume." Table I, A of that memoir gives the vertices of C_{600} with respect to a concentric rectangular system of axes through vertices. We can represent them by means of the following symbols:

$$[2(1+e),\quad 0,\quad 0,\quad 0]\tfrac{1}{2} \quad . \; . \quad 8$$
$$[\;3+e,\; 1+e,\quad 2,\quad 0]\tfrac{1}{2} \quad . \; . \quad 96$$
$$[\;1+e,\; 1+e,\; 1+e,\; 1+e]\tfrac{1}{2} \quad . \; . \quad 16$$

where e stands for $\sqrt{5}$. The length of the edge is 4.

Now table III, A gives the vertices of the T which bound C_{600}. They were determined for the purpose of finding the the centres of these T, which are vertices of a C_{120}. The latter vertices are contained in list C of table III, with respect to a system of axes through bounding D of C_{120}, i. e. exactly our system. So the list C gives the centres of the O which bound the truncated C_{600}. And from the list A we deduce the vertices, edges and faces which bound them.

Table II of the mentioned memoir gives the 12 vertices to which a vertex of C_{600} is joined by edges. It is by determining the midpoints of these edges that we find the vertices of the truncating I. And from the coordinates of the vertices we can deduce those of the edges and faces which bound the I.

In this way we determined all the limits of the polytope, and those of its bounding polyhedra. Of the results we collected what is necessary for our purpose in the following tables.

We have yet to explain the notations appearing in the last columns of our tables A, D and E. The letters represent the even substitions, viz.

---

1) Verhand. Kon. Akad. v. Wetensch. Amsterdam, 1st. section, vol. II, no. 7, 1893.

$$a = (bcd),\quad b = (cda),\quad c = (dab),\quad d = (abc)$$
$$a^2 = (bdc),\quad b^2 = (cad),\quad c^2 = (dba),\quad d^2 = (acb)$$
$$(ab) = (ab)(cd),\quad (ac) = (ac)(bd),\quad (ad) = (ad)(bc).$$

The numerical subscripts indicate the coordinates which have the negative sign. For instance

$$a^2 1_{34}$$

(table E) indicates that the substitution a^2 must be operated on E_1 (of table A) and that afterwards the negative sign must be attributed to the third and fourth coordinates. Hence it indicates the vertex

$$5 + 3e,\ 0,\ -(1+e),\ -2.$$

TABLE A.

(Length of edge = 4).

Vertices	Number	Icosahedra	Octahedra
		through the vertex	
$E_1[5+3e,\ 1+e,\ 2,\ 0]\frac{1}{2}$	96	1, 2	1, 1_4, $a^2 1$, 2, 2_4
$E_2[6+2e,\ 2+2e,\ 0,\ 0]\frac{1}{2}$	48	2, 2_3	1, 1_4, 3, 4, 4_4
$E_3[4+2e,\ 4+2e,\ 2,\ 2]\frac{1}{2}$	96	2, $(ab)2$	3, 4, $(ab)4$, 5, $(ab)5$
$E_4[6+2e,\ 1+e,\ 3+e,\ 2]\frac{1}{2}$	192	2, $a^2 2$	$a^2 1$, 2, $a^2 4$, $a^2 5$, 6
$E_5[4+2e,\ 3+e,\ 5+e,\ 0]\frac{1}{2}$	96	2, $d2$	$a^2 4$, $a^2 5$, $a^2 5_4$, 7, 7_4
$E_6[4+2e,\ 2+2e,\ 3+e,\ 1+e]\frac{1}{2}$	192	2,3	5, $(ab)5$, $a^2 5$, 6, 7

In table D the vertices are placed in this arrangement

1

2 3 4 5

6

where (1, 6), (2, 4) and (3, 5) are pairs of opposite vertices.

In table E the order of the vertices is

a

b *c* *d* *e* *f*

g *h* *i* *j* *k*

l

TABLE B.

(Length of edge = 8).

Edges	Number
K_1 $[10+6e,\ 2+2e,\ 0,\ 0]\frac{1}{2}$	48
K_2 $[11+5e,\ 3+3e,\ 2,\ 0]\frac{1}{2}$	96
K_3 $[10+6e,\ 1+e,\ 3+e,\ 2]\frac{1}{2}$	192
K_4 $[11+5e,\ 2+2e,\ 5+e,\ 2]\frac{1}{2}$	192
K_5 $[11+5e,\ 4+2e,\ 4,\ 1+e]\frac{1}{2}$	192
K_6 $[10+4e,\ 6+4e,\ 2,\ 2]\frac{1}{2}$	192
K_7 $[12+4e,\ 5+3e,\ 2,\ 1+e]\frac{1}{2}$	192
K_8 $[8+4e,\ 8+4e,\ 0,\ 4]\frac{1}{2}$	96
K_9 $[10+4e,\ 7+3e,\ 4,\ 3+e]\frac{1}{2}$	192
K_{10} $[8+4e,\ 9+3e,\ 2,\ 5+e]\frac{1}{2}$	192
K_{11} $[8+4e,\ 6+4e,\ 5+e,\ 3+e]\frac{1}{2}$	192
K_{12} $[12+4e,\ 2+2e,\ 6+2e,\ 0]\frac{1}{2}$	96
K_{13} $[10+4e,\ 4+2e,\ 8+2e,\ 2]\frac{1}{2}$	192
K_{14} $[12+4e,\ 4+2e,\ 5+e,\ 3+e]\frac{1}{2}$	192
K_{15} $[10+4e,\ 3+3e,\ 6+2e,\ 3+e]\frac{1}{2}$	192
K_{16} $[10+4e,\ 2+2e,\ 5+3e,\ 5+e]\frac{1}{2}$	192
K_{17} $[9+3e,\ 7+3e,\ 8+2e,\ 0]\frac{1}{2}$	96
K_{18} $[8+4e,\ 5+3e,\ 8+2e,\ 1+e]\frac{1}{2}$	192
K_{19} $[6+4e,\ 6+2e,\ 9+3e,\ 1+e]\frac{1}{2}$	192
K_{20} $[6+4e,\ 6+4e,\ 4+2e,\ 4+2e]\frac{1}{2}$	96
K_{21} $[8+4e,\ 3+3e,\ 5+3e,\ 4+2e]\frac{1}{2}$	192
K_{22} $[6+4e,\ 5+3e,\ 7+3e,\ 2+2e]\frac{1}{2}$	192

where a and l are opposite vertices, $bcdef$ is the vertex polygon of a and $ghijk$ that of l.

In table A for each vertex have been indicated the O and I which pass through it. This list has been deduced from the tables D and E. They show that the vertex polyhedron

TABLE C.

(Length of edge = 12).

Faces	Number
$F_1\ [16+8e,\ 4+4e,\ 0,\ 0]\frac{1}{2}$	48
$F_2\ [16+8e,\ 2+2e,\ 6+2e,\ 4]\frac{1}{2}$	192
$F_3\ [14+6e,\ 10+6e,\ 0,\ 4]\frac{1}{2}$	96
$F_4\ [18+6e,\ 8+4e,\ 0,\ 2+2e]\frac{1}{2}$	96
$F_5\ [14+6e,\ 12+4e,\ 4,\ 6+2e]\frac{1}{2}$	192
$F_6\ [10+6e,\ 10+6e,\ 6+2e,\ 6+2e]\frac{1}{2}$	96
$F_7\ [18+6e,\ 6+2e,\ 6+2e,\ 6+2e]\frac{1}{2}$	64
$F_8\ [14+6e,\ 4+4e,\ 8+4e,\ 6+2e]\frac{1}{2}$	192
$F_9\ [12+4e,\ 12+4e,\ 12+4e,\ 0]\frac{1}{2}$	32
$F_{10}[10+6e,\ 8+4e,\ 12+4e,\ 2+2e]\frac{1}{2}$	192
$F_{11}[15+9e,\ 4+2e,\ 0,\ 1+e]\frac{1}{2}$	96
$F_{12}[17+7e,\ 6+4e,\ 4,\ 1+e]\frac{1}{2}$	192
$F_{13}[17+7e,\ 8+2e,\ 0,\ 3+3e]\frac{1}{2}$	96
$F_{14}[15+9e,\ 3+e,\ 3+e,\ 3+e]\frac{1}{2}$	64
$F_{15}[17+7e,\ 5+3e,\ 7+e,\ 3+e]\frac{1}{2}$	192
$F_{16}[14+6e,\ 10+6e,\ 4,\ 0]\frac{1}{2}$	96
$F_{17}[16+6e,\ 11+3e,\ 0,\ 5+3e]\frac{1}{2}$	96
$F_{18}[16+6e,\ 9+5e,\ 4,\ 3+e]\frac{1}{2}$	192
$F_{19}[12+6e,\ 13+5e,\ 0,\ 7+e]\frac{1}{2}$	96
$F_{20}[10+6e,\ 9+5e,\ 5+3e,\ 6+4e]\frac{1}{2}$	192
$F_{21}[14+6e,\ 9+5e,\ 7+e,\ 4+2e]\frac{1}{2}$	192
$F_{22}[14+6e,\ 11+3e,\ 3+e,\ 6+4e]\frac{1}{2}$	192
$F_{23}[10+6e,\ 13+5e,\ 3+e,\ 8+2e]\frac{1}{2}$	192
$F_{24}[16+6e,\ 6+4e,\ 8+2e,\ 4+2e]\frac{1}{2}$	192
$F_{25}[12+6e,\ 6+4e,\ 6+4e,\ 6+4e]\frac{1}{2}$	64
$F_{26}[9+5e,\ 9+5e,\ 9+5e,\ 3+3e]\frac{1}{2}$	64
$F_{27}[13+5e,\ 9+5e,\ 11+3e,\ 1+e]\frac{1}{2}$	192

Table D.

(Length of edge = 8).

Octahedra	Number	Vertices
$O_1[11+5e, 4+2e, 0, 1+e]\frac{1}{2}$	96	1 $a1$, $a4$, 2, 1_3 $a4_3$
$O_2[11+5e, 3+e, 3+e, 3+e]\frac{1}{2}$	64	1 $a1$, $a4$, 4, a^21 a^24
$O_3[8+4e, 8+4e, 0, 0]\frac{1}{2}$	24	2 3_4, 3_{34}, 3_3, 3 $(ab)2$
$O_4[10+4e, 7+3e, 0, 3+e]\frac{1}{2}$	96	2 $a4$, $a4_3$, 3_3, 3 $a5$
$O_5[8+4e, 7+3e, 3+e, 4+2e]\frac{1}{2}$	192	3 6, $(ab)6$, $a5$, $a4$ $a6$
$O_6[10+4e, 4+2e, 4+2e, 4+2e]\frac{1}{2}$	64	4 6, a^26, a^24, $a4$ $a6$
$O_7[7+3e, 7+3e, 7+3e, 1+e]\frac{1}{2}$	64	5 6, $d6$, $d5$, d^25 d^26

TABLE E.

(Length of edge = 8).

Icosahedra	Number	Vertices
$I_1[\ 5+3e, \quad 0, \quad 0, \quad 0]_{\frac{1}{2}}$	8	1 $1_3,\ a1, a^21, a^21_4,\ a1_4$ $a^21_3,\ a1_2,\ 1_2,\ a1_{24}, a^21_{34}$ 1_{23}
$I_2[10+4e, 5+3e, 5+\ e, \quad 0]_{\frac{1}{2}}$	96	1 $2,\ a4,\ 4,\ 4_4,\ a4_4$ $3,\ 6,\ 5,\ 6_4,\ 3_4$ d^25
$I_3[\ 5+3e, 5+3e, 5+3e, 5+3e]_{\frac{1}{2}}$	16	6 $a^26, a6, (ab)6, d^26,\ d6$ $c6,\ b6,\ d^26,\ c^26, (ac)6$ $(ad)6$

is bounded by $2p_5$ and $5p_4$ and that it is consequently a P_5. Hence the edges of the polytope are isosceles and equal. Through each edge pass 2 O and 1 I.

All the faces are p_3 but there are two kinds viz. homogeneous ones between two O and heterogeneous ones between an O and an I. We deduce from the structure of the P_5 that the number of heterogeneous faces is twice that of the homogeneous ones.

Hence the polytope has $2\frac{1}{2}$ characteristics of regularity and its degree of regularity is consequently $\frac{5}{8}$.

§ 16. In order to determine the polytope derived from C_{120} by means of truncation as far as the midpoints of the edges we remark that the vertices of that polytope are the centres of the faces of a C_{600} [1]). From table III, A of the memoir mentioned in the preceding art. we derive the vertices, edges, p_3, and T which bound the polytope. They are contained in the tables F, G, H (from F_1 to F_{17} included) and K. From table II of the memoir mentioned we derive the vertices of the truncating ID and hence their centres and their bounding p_5. Table L gives the vertices of the ID in the following arrangement:

(ab) (ac) (ad) (ae) (af)
(bc) (cd) (de) (ef) (fb)
(kb) (bg) (gc) (ch) (hd) (di) (ie) (ej) (jf) (fk)
(kg) (gh) (hi) (ij) (jk)
(lg) (lh) (li) (lj) (lk)

TABLE F.

(Length of edge = 4).

Vertices	Number	T	ID
		through the vertex	
E_1 $[8+4e, 2+2e, 0, 0]\frac{1}{2}$	96	1, 1_4	1, 2, 2_3
E_2 $[8+4e, 1+e, 3+e, 2]\frac{1}{2}$	192	a^21, 2	1, 2, a^22
E_3 $[7+3e, 5+3e, 0, 2]\frac{1}{2}$	96	3, 4	2, 2_3, $(ab)2$
E_4 $[9+3e, 4+2e, 0, 1+e]\frac{1}{2}$	96	1, 4	2, 4_3, $a2$
E_5 $[7+3e, 6+2e, 2, 3+e]\frac{1}{2}$	192	4, 5	2, $a2$, $(ab)2$
E_6 $[5+3e, 5+3e, 3+e, 3+e]\frac{1}{2}$	96	5, $(ab)5$	2, $(ab)2$, 3
E_7 $[9+3e, 3+e, 3+e, 3+e]\frac{1}{2}$	64	2, 6	2, $a2$, a^22
E_8 $[7+3e, 2+2e, 4+2e, 3+e]\frac{1}{2}$	192	a^25, 6	2, a^22, 3
E_9 $[6+2e, 6+2e, 6+2e, 0]\frac{1}{2}$	32	7, 7_4	2, $d2$, d^22
E_{10} $[5+3e, 4+2e, 6+2e, 1+e]\frac{1}{2}$	192	a^25, 7	2, $d10$, 3

1) Mrs. A. BOOLE STOTT and Dr. P. H. SCHOUTE, Proceedings Amsterdam, vol. X, 502.

The letters refer to the vertices of a C_{600} in the arrangement of page 24, and two letters between ( ) indicate the midpoint of the corresponding edge.

The bounding p_5 are the F_{18} to F_{23} of table H.

We can deduce from the tables K and L the T and ID

TABLE G.

(Length of edge = 8).

Edges	Number
K_1 [16 + 8e, 5 + 3e, 2, 1 + e]$\frac{1}{2}$	192
K_2 [17 + 7e, 6 + 4e, 0, 1 + e]$\frac{1}{2}$	96
K_3 [16 + 8e, 6 + 2e, 0, 2 + 2e]$\frac{1}{2}$	96
K_4 [17 + 7e, 7 + 3e, 2, 2 + 2e]$\frac{1}{2}$	192
K_5 [16 + 8e, 5 + e, 3 + e, 4 + 2e]$\frac{1}{2}$	192
K_6 [17 + 7e, 6 + 2e, 5 + e, 4 + 2e]$\frac{1}{2}$	192
K_7 [14 + 6e, 10 + 6e, 0, 0]$\frac{1}{2}$	48
K_8 [12 + 6e, 12 + 6e, 2, 2]$\frac{1}{2}$	96
K_9 [16 + 6e, 9 + 5e, 0, 3 + e]$\frac{1}{2}$	96
K_{10}[14 + 6e, 11 + 5e, 2, 5 + e]$\frac{1}{2}$	192
K_{11}[16 + 6e, 10 + 4e, 2, 4 + 2e]$\frac{1}{2}$	192
K_{12}[14 + 6e, 12 + 4e, 0, 6 + 2e]$\frac{1}{2}$	96
K_{13}[12 + 6e, 11 + 5e, 5 + e, 6 + 2e]$\frac{1}{2}$	192
K_{14}[14 + 6e, 10 + 4e, 5 + e, 5 + 3e]$\frac{1}{2}$	192
K_{15}[12 + 6e, 12 + 4e, 3 + e, 7 + 3e]$\frac{1}{2}$	192
K_{16}[12 + 6e, 9 + 5e, 6 + 2e, 5 + 3e]$\frac{1}{2}$	192
K_{17}[10 + 6e, 11 + 5e, 4 + 2e, 7 + 3e]$\frac{1}{2}$	192
K_{18}[12 + 6e, 10 + 4e, 4 + 2e, 6 + 4e]$\frac{1}{2}$	192
K_{19}[16 + 6e, 5 + 3e, 7 + 3e, 6 + 2e]$\frac{1}{2}$	192
K_{20}[14 + 6e, 6 + 4e, 7 + 3e, 5 + 3e]$\frac{1}{2}$	192
K_{21}[11 + 5e, 10 + 4e, 12 + 4e, 1 + e]$\frac{1}{2}$	192
K_{22}[11 + 5e, 9 + 5e, 10 + 4e, 2 + 2e]$\frac{1}{2}$	192

Table H.

(Length of edge $= 12$).

	Faces	Number
Triangles (2400)	$F_1\,[25+11e,\ 10+4e,\ 0,\ 3+3e]\frac{1}{2}$	96
	$F_2\,[25+11e,\ 9+5e,\ 2,\ 2+2e]\frac{1}{2}$	192
	$F_3\,[24+12e,\ 8+4e,\ 0,\ 2+2e]\frac{1}{2}$	96
	$F_4\,[25+11e,\ 6+2e,\ 7+3e,\ 8+2e]\frac{1}{2}$	192
	$F_5\,[24+12e,\ 6+2e,\ 6+2e,\ 6+2e]\frac{1}{2}$	64
	$F_6\,[19+9e,\ 17+9e,\ 2,\ 0]\frac{1}{2}$	96
	$F_7\,[23+9e,\ 16+6e,\ 0,\ 7+3e]\frac{1}{2}$	96
	$F_8\,[21+9e,\ 17+7e,\ 0,\ 8+2e]\frac{1}{2}$	96
	$F_9\,[23+9e,\ 15+7e,\ 2,\ 6+2e]\frac{1}{2}$	192
	$F_{10}[17+9e,\ 15+7e,\ 7+3e,\ 9+5e]\frac{1}{2}$	192
	$F_{11}[19+9e,\ 16+6e,\ 6+2e,\ 9+5e]\frac{1}{2}$	192
	$F_{12}[17+9e,\ 17+7e,\ 6+2e,\ 10+4e]\frac{1}{2}$	192
	$F_{13}[19+9e,\ 15+7e,\ 8+2e,\ 8+4e]\frac{1}{2}$	192
	$F_{14}[21+9e,\ 9+5e,\ 9+5e,\ 9+5e]\frac{1}{2}$	64
	$F_{15}[23+9e,\ 10+4e,\ 8+4e,\ 9+5e]\frac{1}{2}$	192
	$F_{16}[15+7e,\ 15+7e,\ 15+7e,\ 3+3e]\frac{1}{2}$	64
	$F_{17}[16+6e,\ 17+7e,\ 15+7e,\ 2+2e]\frac{1}{2}$	192
Pentagons (720)	$F_{18}[40+20e,\ 10+6e,\ 10+2e,\ 0]\frac{1}{2}$	96
	$F_{19}[40+16e,\ 20+12e,\ 0,\ 0]\frac{1}{2}$	48
	$F_{20}[40+16e,\ 20+8e,\ 10+2e,\ 10+6e]\frac{1}{2}$	192
	$F_{21}[30+14e,\ 30+14e,\ 10+2e,\ 10+2e]\frac{1}{2}$	96
	$F_{22}[30+14e,\ 20+12e,\ 20+8e,\ 10+6e]\frac{1}{2}$	192
	$F_{23}[30+10e,\ 30+14e,\ 20+8e,\ 0]\frac{1}{2}$	96

which pass through any vertex. They are represented in table F. So we find that the vertex polyhedron is a 3-angular prism, the lateral edges of which are $=\frac{1}{2}(e+1)$, and

TABLE K.

(Length of edge $= \frac{16}{3}$).

Tetrahedra	Number	Vertices
$T_1[11+5e,\ 4+2e,\ 0,\ 1+e]\frac{1}{2}$	96	1, $a2$, $a2_3$, 4
$T_2[11+5e,\ 3+e,\ 3+e,\ 3+e]\frac{1}{2}$	64	$a2$, a^22, 2, 7
$T_3[8+4e,\ 8+4e,\ 0,\ 0]\frac{1}{2}$	24	3, 3, $(ab)3$, $(ab)3_3$
$T_4[10+4e,\ 7+3e,\ 0,\ 3+e]\frac{1}{2}$	96	3, 4, 5, 5_3
$T_5[8+4e,\ 7+3e,\ 3+e,\ 4+2e]\frac{1}{2}$	192	5, 6, $a8$, $a10$
$T_6[10+4e,\ 4+2e,\ 4+2e,\ 4+2e]\frac{1}{2}$	64	7, 8, $a8$, a^28
$T_7[7+3e,\ 7+3e,\ 7+3e,\ 1+e]\frac{1}{2}$	64	9, 10, $d10$, d^210

TABLE L.

(Length of edge = 4).

ID	Vertices
$ID_1[8+4e, 0, 0, 0]\frac{1}{2}$ (8)	1 $a2$ 2 2_4 $a2_4$ $a2_3$ a^22 a^21 a^22_4 $a2_{34}$ 2_{34} 2_3 a^22_3 $a1$ a^22_2 2_2 2_{24} a^22_{24} $a1_4$ a^22_{34} a^21_3 a^22_{23} $a2_2$ $a2_{24}$ a^22_{234} 2_{23} $a2_{23}$ 1_2 $a2_{234}$ 2_{234}
$ID_2[7+3e, 4+2e, 3+e, 0]\frac{1}{2}$ (96)	1 $a2$ 2 2_4 $a2_4$ 4 7 a^24 7_4 4_4 3_4 3 5 $a8$ 8 a^25 a^25_4 8_4 $a8_4$ 5_4 $(ab)3$ 6 10 10_4 6_4 $(ab)5$ d^210 9 d^210_4 $(ab)5_4$
$ID_3[4+2e, 4+2e, 4+2e, 4+2e]\frac{1}{2}$ (16)	8 $a8$ 6 d^210 10 a^28 $a10$ d^28 $d10$ a^26 $(ac)10$ a^210 $a6$ $b10$ $(ab)10$ $(ab)8$ c^28 d^26 $d8$ $(ac)8$ $c10$ $b8$ $b6$ c^210 b^28 $c8$ $(ad)8$ $(ad)10$ b^210 $(ac)6$

those of the bases = 1, in terms of the edge of the polytope as unit.

Hence the edges of the polytope are isosceles and equal. Through each edge pass 2 ID and 1 T.

The bounding p_3 are equal and heterogeneous (between ID and T), the p_5 are equal and homogeneous (between two ID). We deduce from the structure of the vertex polyhedron that the number of heterogeneous faces is twice that of the homogeneous ones.

Hence the polytope has 2 characteristics of regularity. Its degree of regularity is consequently $\frac{1}{2}$.

Summary. § 17. The following table contains the five polytopes derived from the regular cells by means of truncation as far as the midpoints of the edges. Their notations correspond to those of the cell from which they are derived.

D means "degree of regularity".

Notation	E	K	F	R	Through an edge	Through a vertex	D
tC_5	10	30	10 + 20	5 + 5	2O + 1T	3O + 2T	$\frac{5}{8}$
tC_8	32	96	24 + 64	8 + 16	2CO + 1T	3CO + 2T	$\frac{1}{2}$
tC_{24}	96	288	96 + 144	24 + 24	2CO + 1C	3CO + 2C	$\frac{1}{2}$
tC_{600}	720	3600	1200 + 2400	600 + 120	2O + 1I	5O + 2I	$\frac{5}{8}$
tC_{120}	1200	3600	720 + 2400	120 + 600	2ID + 1T	3ID + 2T	$\frac{1}{2}$

The reciprocal polars of the polytopes. § 18. To any of the mentioned polytopes corresponds a polar. It may be constructed by bringing through the vertices threedimensional spaces tangent to the circumscribing spherical space. The statements made for any of the preceding cells will hold for its polar after applying a kind of translation where "vertex" and "bounding space", "equally long edges" and "equal angles between spaces", etc. etc. interchange. Hence we can dispense with an elaborate investigation of the polar polytopes and confine ourselves to the following remarks.

The regularity is of the second kind, and the degree is equal to that of the polar polytope of the first kind.

The bounding space is dualistically related (in *three*dimensional duality) to the vertex polyhedron of the corresponding polytope of the first kind. Indeed the vertices, edges and faces of the bounding space correspond to the spaces, faces and edges passing through the vertex of the polar polytope of the first kind, and consequently to the faces, edges and vertices of its vertex polyhedron. In consequence the bounding spaces are successively:

3-angular bipyramids having the degree of regularity $\frac{1}{2}$,
3- " " " " " " " $\frac{1}{3}$,
3- " " " " " " " $\frac{1}{3}$,
5- " " " " " " " $\frac{1}{2}$,
3- " " " " " " " $\frac{1}{3}$.

In the same way the face is dualistically related (in *two*-dimensional duality) to the edge polygon of the polar polytope of the first kind.

Construction of these polytopes

§ 19. The polytopes of the second kind are immediately derivable from the regular cells by means of the following construction. On the bounding spaces of the regular cell place regular and equal pyramids of such height that two lateral spaces meeting at a face of the cell are situated in one space. But this operation must be applied to the regular cell which corresponds dualistically to the cell from which the polar polytope of the first kind was derived by the operation t.

An other construction by which to obtain them consists in passing spaces through each edge of a regular cell making equal angles with the bounding spaces through that edge. This construction must be applied to the same regular cell as that from which the polar polytope is derived by the operation t.

CHAPTER III.

NEW FOURDIMENSIONAL SEMIREGULAR POLYTOPES OF THE FIRST KIND.

nvestigation the semire- ar polyto- s bounded regular po- edra only.

§ 20. We will now endeavour to find the other polytopes in S_4 the degree of regularity of which is $\frac{1}{2}$ or more, and we begin our investigation by finding those bounded by regular polyhedra only. We have only to consider T, O and I.

The sum of the dihedral angles of polyhedra through an edge must be less than 360°; the sum of the solid angles in the polyhedra meeting at a vertex must be less than 720°. In consequence of the former condition we have to examine the following cases (consult list of angles, page 10):

I. T + 2O through an edge.

Let x represent the number of edges through a vertex of the polytope, then through a vertex pass

$$\frac{x}{3}\mathrm{T} + \frac{x}{2}\mathrm{O}.$$

Let e, k and f represent the numbers of vertices, edges and faces of the vertex polyhedron, then $e = x$. Through a vertex pass 3 faces corresponding to the 3 spaces through an edge of the polytope. Consequently $k = \frac{3}{2}x$. The faces are $\frac{x}{3}$ triangles and $\frac{x}{2}$ squares. Hence by EULER's theorem

$$x - \frac{3}{2}x + \frac{x}{3} + \frac{x}{2} = 2,$$

$$x = 6.$$

Through a vertex pass $2T + 3O$. This case is nothing else than tC_5.

II. $2T + O$ through an edge.

Through a vertex $\frac{2}{3}\,xT + \frac{1}{4}\,xO$,

$$e = x,\ k = \tfrac{3}{2}\,x,\ f = \tfrac{2}{3} + \tfrac{1}{4}.$$

From EULER's theorem results

$$x = \tfrac{24}{5}$$

which is to be rejected.

III. $3T + O$ through an edge.

Through a vertex pass $xT + \frac{1}{4}\,xO$,

$$e = x,\ k = 2x,\ f = \tfrac{1}{4}\,x + x.$$

By EULER's theorem $x = 8$.

The vertex polyhedron is AP_4. Through a vertex of the polytope pass $8T + 2O$. The sum of the solid angles is about 402°.

We will demonstrate that this case is yet to be rejected. As in AP_4 a triangle is enclosed by two triangles and a square, two of the three faces through the vertex of a T are covered by other T, the third by an O. This cannot be realized for all the vertices of a T.

IV. $2O + I$ through an edge.

Trough a vertex pass $\frac{x}{2}\,O + \frac{x}{5}\,I$,

$$e = x,\ k = \frac{3}{2}\,x,\ f = \frac{x}{2} + \frac{x}{5}.$$

By EULER's theorem $x = 10$.

The vertex polyhedron is P_5, so the polytope is tC_{600}.

V. $2T + I$ through an edge.

Through a vertex $\frac{2}{3}\,xT + \frac{1}{5}\,xI$,

$$e = x,\ k = \frac{3}{2}\,x,\ f = \frac{2}{3}\,x + \frac{x}{5}.$$

By EULER's theorem $x = \frac{60}{11}$ which must be rejected.

VI. $3T + I$ through an edge.

Through a vertex $xT + \frac{1}{5}\,xI$.

By EULER's theorem $x = 10$.

The vertex polyhedron is AP_5. By a similar reasoning as for III we are able to prove that the polytope does not exist.

VII. $T + O + I$ through an edge.

Through a vertex $\frac{x}{3}T + \frac{x}{4}O + \frac{x}{5}I$.

By EULER's theorem $x = \frac{120}{17}$, which cannot be realized. So there are no other semiregular polytopes bounded by regular polyhedra only than tC_5 and tC_{600}.

Investigation of the semiregular polytopes bounded by regular and semiregular polyhedra.

§ 21. We will now admit semiregular polyhedra among the bounding spaces.

In tT, tC, tO, tD, tI and P_n ($P_4 = C$ excluded) the number of heterogeneous edges is $\frac{2}{3}k$, the number of homogeneous ones is $\frac{1}{3}k$, k being the total number of edges. The dihedral angle at a homogeneous edge is different from that at a heterogeneous edge. Now let one of the mentioned polyhedra appear among the bounding spaces of a polytope whose degree of regularity is at least $\frac{1}{2}$. Let $(p + q)$ polyhedra pass through an edge, while that edge is heterogeneous edge in p, homogeneous in q of these polyhedra. Then the polyhedron appears to the number of

$$\frac{Kp}{\frac{2}{3}k} = \frac{Kq}{\frac{1}{3}k}.$$

Hence $p = 2q$.

For $q = 2$, and consequently $p = 4$, the sum of the dihedral angles at an edge is more than 360° for any of the mentioned polytopes. For $q = 1$, $p = 2$, that sum is less than 360° for tT, tC and P_n. With regard to the given reasoning it is of no consequence whether the polytope is bounded by one kind of the mentioned semiregulars or by one kind in connection with an other.

Thus we have to expect polytopes bounded by tT, tC or P_n.

Through an edge pass 3 tT. Through a vertex pass x tT. For the vertex polyhedron we have

$$e = x, \quad k = \tfrac{3}{2}x, \quad f = x.$$

Hence, by EULER's theorem $x = 4$. Through a vertex pass 4 tT.

Through an edge pass 3 tC. Through a vertex pass x tC,

$$e = x, \quad k = \tfrac{3}{2}x, \quad f = x.$$

By EULER's theorem $x = 4$. Through a vertex pass 4 tC.

Through an edge pass 3 P_n. Through a vertex pass x P_n,

$$e = x, \quad k = \tfrac{3}{2}x, \quad f = x.$$

By EULER's theorem $x = 4$. Through a vertex pass 4 P_n.

We will demonstrate in the pages that follow that these polytopes exist. But we will now examine whether there is still room for an other polyhedron.

In the case of tT the sum of the dihedral angles is 289° 28′ 17″. So addition of the smallest dihedral angle, that of T, just fills 360°.

In the case of tC the sum of the dihedral angles is about 340°.

In the case of P_3 the sum of angles is 240°. Thus we have to consider:

$$3P_3 + T,$$
$$3P_3 + C,$$
$$3P_3 + O$$

through an edge.

$3P_3 + 1T$. Through a vertex pass $\frac{x}{3}$ T $+ x P_3$. For the vertex polyhedron we have $e = x$, $k = 2x$, $f = \frac{x}{3} + \frac{x}{4}$.

Hence by EULER's theorem $x = 6$.

The vertex polyhedron is a 3-angular antiprism whose degree of regularity is $\frac{1}{3}$. The edges of the bases are 1, the lateral edges $\sqrt{2}$ (1 = edge of polytope). The polytope exists and will be considered more thoroughly.

$3P_3 + 1C$. Through a vertex pass $x\,P_3 + \frac{x}{3}\,C$,

$$e = x, \quad k = 2x, \quad f = x + \frac{x}{3}$$

By EULER's theorem $\quad x = 6$.

Through a vertex pass $6\ P_3 + 2C$ whose sum of solid angles is 540°. The vertex polyhedron is a 3-angular antiprism, whose degree of regularity is $\frac{1}{3}$. The edges of the bases are $\sqrt{2}$, the lateral edges 1 and $\sqrt{2}$ alternately ($1 =$ edge of polytope). Hence a lateral face has one of its sides $\sqrt{2}$ in common with a base of the antiprism, the two other sides with other lateral faces. That means that of the three faces passing through a vertex of P_3 the triangle and one of the squares are covered by other P_3, while the remaining square is covered by a C. As this cannot be realized for all the vertices of a P_3 this case must be rejected.

$3P_3 + 1O$. Through a vertex pass $x\,P_3 + \frac{x}{4}\,O$,

$$e = x, \quad k = 2x, \quad f = x + \frac{x}{4}.$$

By EULER's theorem $x = 8$.

The vertex polyhedron is a 4-angular antiprism whose degree of regularity is $\frac{1}{3}$. The bases are squares whose sides are 1, the lateral edges are $\sqrt{2}$ ($1 =$ edge of polytope). This polytope exists and will be examined more closely.

In the case of $3\,P_5$ through an edge the sum of dihedral angles is 288°. There is room for one T, which must be rejected as it does not suit the squares and pentagons of P_5.

We need not consider other cases of P_n.

It is impossible to bound a polytope by means of either CO or ID only. Indeed, as through an edge of these pass two different faces, through an edge of the polytope must pass an even number of these polyhedra, consequently at least 4. Then the sum of angles is more than 360°.

But we can make to pass through an edge 2CO (sum of angles $= 250° 31' 43''$) and try to add an other polyhedron. We have to consider:

2 CO + 1T. Through a vertex pass $\frac{x}{2}$ CO + $\frac{x}{3}$ T,

$$e = x, \quad k = \frac{3}{2} x, \quad f = \frac{x}{2} + \frac{x}{3}.$$

By EULER's theorem $x = 6$. This polytope is tC_8.

2 CO + 1C. Through a vertex pass $\frac{x}{2}$ CO + $\frac{x}{3}$ C,

$$e = x, \; k = \frac{3}{2} x, \; f = \frac{x}{2} + \frac{x}{3}$$

By EULER's theorem $x = 6$. This polytope is tC_{24}.

In the same way we have to consider 2 ID + 1T through an edge. This is nothing else than tC_{120}.

In RCO and RID there are two kinds of edges, both heterogeneous and equal in number. Hence we cannot bound a polytope by either of them, for that would require 4 spaces through an edge.

In the case of 2 RID through an edge the sum of angles is about 300°, so we cannot combine them with an other polyhedron.

This might succeed with 2 RCO, where there is a remainder of about 80°. But the two RCO have a square in common (and not a triangle, for then two equal angles would meet at an edge), so that a square and a triangle are yet uncovered. That would suit only P_3 and this only appears in triplets.

In tCO and tID there are three kinds of edges equal in number. Thus they can only appear in threefolds through an edge. The sum of angles is by far too great.

In CS and DS there are two kinds of edges as to their number in the ratio 2 : 3. Hence they can only appear in fivefolds through an edge. Their angles are too great for that.

In AP_n there are two kinds of edges, equal in number. Thus, in order to bound a polytope by one kind of AP_n we have to pass at least 4 AP_n through an edge. Then the sum of angles is more than 360°. Indeed the angle between two lateral faces is about 109° for $n = 3$ and increases with n. The angle between a lateral face and a base decreases when n increases, but is always more than 90°.

We will now consider 2 AP_n through an edge and try to add an other polyhedron.

$AP_3 = O$ has been considered among the regulars.

2 AP_4 through an edge leave about 129° and then a triangle and a square are yet uncovered. Thus we might try to add 1 CO. (This supposition is *not* incompatible with what we stated before, viz. that only an *even* number of CO can be admitted. Compare the reason for that statement). But this cannot be realized as the number of squares and triangles is unequal in CO.

2 AP_5 leave about 121°, and a triangle and a pentagon are uncovered. That would fit ID, whose angle is too great.

The remaining AP_n need not be considered.

The result of this investigation is, that, besides the polytopes described in Chapter II, we have to consider:

	Through an edge	Through a vertex
I	3tT	4tT
II	3tC	4tC
III	$3P_3 + 1T$	$6P_3 + 2T$
IV	$3P_3 + 1O$	$6P_3 + 2O$
V	$3P_n$	$4P_n$.

(30, 60, 40, 10). § 22. The vertex polyhedron in case I is a tetrahedron, two opposite edges of which are 1, the other $\sqrt{3}$ (1 = edge of polytope).

Hence $K = 2E$, $F = \frac{4}{3}E$, $R = \frac{1}{3}E$. We cannot calculate E by means of EULER's theorem, as this furnishes a *homogeneous* equation. So we have to try other methods.

We begin by determining the radius r_u of the circumscribed spherical space in terms of the edge. This radius is for the vertex polyhedron

$$\varrho = \frac{1}{4}\sqrt{14}.$$

Hence $$r_u = \sqrt{2}.$$

Then we calculate the following lengthes:

Radius of circumscribed sphere of tT $= r_1 = \dfrac{\sqrt{22}}{4}$.

Distance from centre of polytope to the centre of tT $= r_2 = \dfrac{1}{4}\sqrt{10}$.

Distance from centre of tT to the centre of a bounding hexagon $= r_3 = \dfrac{1}{4}\sqrt{6}$.

Distance from centre of tT to that of a bounding triangle $= r_4 = \dfrac{5}{12}\sqrt{6}$.

Let φ be the angle between the lines that join the centre of the polytope to the centres of two tT having a hexagon in common, and ψ the corresponding angle for two tT having a triangle in common. Then

$$\left.\begin{aligned} \tan\frac{1}{2}\varphi = \frac{r_3}{r_2} = \sqrt{\frac{3}{5}} \\ \tan\varphi = \sqrt{15} \\ \cos\varphi = \frac{1}{4} \end{aligned}\right\}, \qquad \left.\begin{aligned} \tan\frac{1}{2}\psi = \frac{r_4}{r_2} = \sqrt{\frac{5}{3}} \\ \tan\psi = -\sqrt{15} \\ \cos\psi = -\frac{1}{4} \end{aligned}\right\}.$$

Hence ψ is exactly the angle between two vertex radii (or between two space radii) of C_5, and φ is the angle between a vertex radius and an adjacent space radius [1]). Hence we are justified to expect that the bounding spaces of the present

---

[1]) P. H. SCHOUTE, Mehrdimensionale Geometrie II, pag. 233.

cell correspond to the vertices and faces of C_5 and that it may be derived by truncation. If this is possible we have to expect that two truncating spaces and that two truncated spaces have a triangle in common, whilst a truncating and a truncated space have a hexagon in common.

In order to prove the existence of the polytope let A_1, A_2, A_3, A_4 and A_5 be the vertices of a C_5, and let us consider the vertex polyhedron of A_1, i. e. the opposite T. In this T we

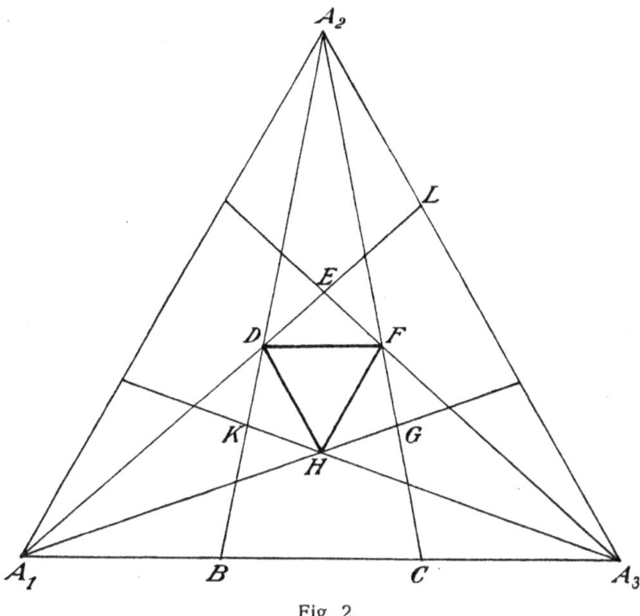

Fig. 2.

can construct a tT by determining on each edge three points dividing the edge into three equal segments. Then joining these points to A_1 by means of straight lines and determining on these lines points at equal distance from A_1, these points limit a similar tT, which truncates C_5. If we do the same for the other vertex polyhedra, the joining lines enclose in each face of C_5 a hexagon, as shown in fig. 2. Now, the alternate vertices D, F and H, and their analoga in the other faces are the vertices of our cell. As far as the truncating spaces are concerned it results from the preceding reasoning. As to the truncated spaces, it may be demonstrated by means of elementary geometry that the T of C_5 is, in this way, transformed into tT.

The C_5 is truncated as far as $\frac{3}{5}$ of the edge. For in fig. 2

$$A_2D : DB = 3 : 2.$$

We will now examine the polytope more closely.

The vertex H will be denoted by $E_{1(2)3}$, the indices being those of the face of C_5 in which the vertex is situated, the ( ) round 2 indicating that the vertex is opposite to A_2. Their number is 30.

This vertex is joined by edges to $E_{(1)23}$ and $E_{12(3)}$ in the same face of C_5; moreover to the two vertices $E_{13(4)}$ and $E_{13(5)}$ situated in the two other faces of C_5 through the edge A_1A_3. We want two notations for the edges. The edge through $E_{1(2)3}$ and $E_{(1)23}$ will be represented by $K_{(1)(2)3}$,

" " " $E_{1(2)3}$ " $E_{13(4)}$ " " " " $K_{1(2)3(4)}$.

Their numbers are $(5)_3 \,.\, (3)_2 = 30$ and $(5)_4 \,.\, (4)_2 = 30$ respectively. Thus $K = 60$.

We will represent the faces which coincide with those of C_5 by the notation of the latter (art. 12). Thus

$$F_{\overline{4}\overline{5}}$$

s limited by

$$\left.\begin{matrix} E_{(1)23} \\ E_{1(2)3} \\ E_{12(3)} \end{matrix}\right\} \text{ and } \left.\begin{matrix} K_{1(2)(3)} \\ K_{(1)2(3)} \\ K_{(1)(2)3} \end{matrix}\right\}.$$

Their number is 10.

Then there are faces which are wholly limited by edges of the second kind, e.g. $K_{12(3)(4)}$, $K_{12(3)(5)}$ and $K_{12(4)(5)}$. We will represent this face by F_{12}. Their number is 10, and they correspond to the edges of C_5. Indeed they belong to pairs of truncating spaces.

The hexagons are the truncating faces of the tT. Like in art. 12 we will denote the hexagon that is situated in $T_{\overset{-}{5}}$ near the vertex E_2 by $F_{\overset{+}{2}\overset{-}{5}}$. It is limited by the vertices

$$E_{(1)23},\quad E_{12(3)},\quad E_{12(4)},\quad E_{(1)24},\quad E_{2(3)4},\quad E_{23(4)}.$$

The spaces will be represented by indices corresponding to the vertices and spaces of C_5.

Thus the truncating

$$tT_{\overset{+}{2}}$$

is bounded by

the triangles F_{12}, F_{23}, F_{24}, F_{25},
the hexagons $F_{\overset{-}{1}\overset{+}{2}}$, $F_{\overset{+}{2}\overset{-}{3}}$, $F_{\overset{+}{2}\overset{-}{4}}$, $F_{\overset{+}{2}\overset{-}{5}}$.

The truncated

$$tT_{\overset{-}{2}}$$

is limited by

the triangles $F_{\overset{-}{1}\overset{-}{2}}$, $F_{\overset{-}{2}\overset{-}{3}}$, $F_{\overset{-}{2}\overset{-}{4}}$, $F_{\overset{-}{2}\overset{-}{5}}$,
the hexagons $F_{\overset{+}{1}\overset{-}{2}}$, $F_{\overset{-}{2}\overset{+}{3}}$, $F_{\overset{-}{2}\overset{+}{4}}$, $F_{\overset{-}{2}\overset{+}{5}}$.

We will now compare the bounding elements.

The triangles are equal.

Through $F_{\overset{-}{4}\overset{-}{5}}$ pass $tT_{\overset{-}{4}}$ and $tT_{\overset{-}{5}}$,
" F_{23} " $tT_{\overset{+}{2}}$ " $tT_{\overset{+}{3}}$.

The hexagons are equal.

Through $F_{\overset{+}{2}\overset{-}{3}}$ pass $tT_{\overset{+}{3}}$ and $tT_{\overset{-}{3}}$.

All the faces are homogeneous. The dihedral angles at a triangle and at a hexagon are the supplements of ψ and φ.

The edges are equal.

Through $K_{(1)(2)3}$ pass $F_{\overset{-}{4}\overset{-}{5}}$, $F_{\overset{+}{3}\overset{-}{4}}$, $F_{\overset{+}{3}\overset{-}{5}}$ and $tT_{\overset{-}{4}}$, $tT_{\overset{-}{5}}$, $tT_{\overset{+}{3}}$,
" $K_{12(3)(4)}$ " F_{12}, $F_{\overset{+}{1}\overset{-}{5}}$, $F_{\overset{+}{2}\overset{-}{5}}$ " $tT_{\overset{+}{1}}$, $tT_{\overset{+}{2}}$, $tT_{\overset{-}{5}}$.

They are isosceles.

The degree of regularity of the polytope is $\frac{1}{2}$.

(288, 576, 336, 48). § 23. We will now apply the operation by means of which we derived the preceding polytope from C_5 to the other regular cells. Perhaps the result may answer any of the cases mentioned at the end of art. 23.

The bounding spaces are

for C_8 :	truncating tC,	truncated tO,	
„ C_{16} :	„ tO,	„ tT,	
„ C_{24} :	„ tC,	„ tC,	
„ C_{600} :	„ tI,	„ tT,	
„ C_{120} :	„ tT,	„ tI	

Thus it appears that the truncation of C_{24} will lead to case II. We found for that case that the vertex polyhedron is a tetrahedron. Through a vertex pass 4tC. Two opposite edges of the vertex polyhedron are 1, the other $2+\sqrt{2}$ ($1=$ edge of polytope).

Here again we begin by transforming a vertex polyhedron of C_{24} i. e. C into tC. For this purpose we determine on each edge two points at a distance $\frac{1}{2}(2-\sqrt{2})$ ($1=$ edge of C_{24}) from the limiting vertices. Then we proceed as with C_5.

The truncation reaches as far as $(2-\sqrt{2})$ times the edge of C_{24}.

Let $F[\frac{4}{3}, \frac{4}{3}, \frac{4}{3}, 0]$ be the homogeneous faces of C_{24} (art. 14), bounded by

$$E[2, 2, 0, 0], \quad E[2, 0, 2, 0], \quad E[0, 2, 2, 0];$$

then the coordinates of the vertices of the derived polytope situated in these faces are

$$[\sqrt{2}, 1, 1, 0], \quad [1, \sqrt{2}, 1, 0], \quad [1, 1, \sqrt{2}, 0].$$

Here we have one kind of vertex, which will be represented by

$$E_1[2p, 1, 1, 0],$$

where p stands for $\frac{1}{2}\sqrt{2}$. Their number is 96.

In the quasi-heterogeneous faces

$$F[2, \tfrac{2}{3}, \tfrac{2}{3}, \tfrac{2}{3}]$$

bounded by

$$E[2,\ 2,\ 0,\ 0], \quad E[2,\ 0,\ 2,\ 0], \quad E[2,\ 0,\ 0,\ 2]$$

we find

$E_2[1+p, 1-p, p, p], E_2[1+p, p, 1-p, p], E_2[1+p, p, p, 1-p]$

The number of this kind of vertices is 192. Thus $E = 288$.

The length of the edge of C_{24} is, in the notation of art. 14, equal to $\sqrt{2}$. The edge of the derived polytope is $6 - 4\sqrt{2}$. Hence we have to find the vertices having that distance from a given vertex. So we get edges from

$$E_1[2p,\ 1,\ 1,\ 0]$$

to

$E_1[1, 2p, 1, 0], E_1[1, 1, 2p, 0], E_2[1+p, p, p, 1-p], E_2[1+p, p, p, p-1]$;

and from

$$E_2[1+p,\ 1-p,\ p,\ p]$$

to

$E_2[1+p, p, 1-p, p], E_2[1+p, p, p, 1-p], E_2[1+p, p-1, p, p], E_1[2p, 0, 1, 1]$.

We have four notations for the edges

$K_1[2p+1, 2p+1, 2, 0]$	through $E_1[2p, 1, 1, 0]$	and	$E_1[1, 2p, 1, 0]$,
$K_2[3p+1, p+1, p+1, 1-p]$	„ $E_1[2p, 1, 1, 0]$	„	$E_2[1+p, p, p, 1-p]$,
$K_3[2p+2, 1, 1, 2p]$	„ $E_2[1+p, 1-p, p, p]$	„	$E_2[1+p, p, 1-p, p]$,
$K_4[2p+2, 0, 2p, 2p]$	„ $E_2[1+p, 1-p, p, p]$	„	$E_2[1+p, p-1, p, p]$.

So $K = 96 + 192 + 192 + 96 = 576$.

The faces are partly triangles.

$F_1[2p+2,\ 2p+2,\ 2p+2,\ 0]$

bounded by

$$\left.\begin{matrix} E_1[1,\ 1,\ 2p,\ 0] \\ E_1[2p,\ 1,\ 1,\ 0] \\ E_1[1,\ 2p,\ 1,\ 0] \end{matrix}\right\} \text{ and } \left.\begin{matrix} K_1[2p+1,\ 2p+1,\ 2,\ 0] \\ K_1[2,\ 2p+1,\ 2p+1,\ 0] \\ K_1[2p+1,\ 2,\ 2p+1,\ 0] \end{matrix}\right\}.$$

Their number is 32 and through any K_1 passes one F_1.

They correspond to the homogeneous faces $F[\frac{4}{3}, \frac{4}{3}, \frac{4}{3}, 0]$ of C_{24}.

The face $F_2[4p+2,\ 2p+1,\ 2p+1,\ 0]$ is bounded by

$$\left.\begin{matrix} E_1[2p,\ 1,\ 1,\ 0] \\ E_2[1+p,\ p,\ p,\ 1-p] \\ E_2[1+p,\ p,\ p,\ p-1] \end{matrix}\right\} \text{ and } \left.\begin{matrix} K_4[2p+2,\ 2p,\ 2p,\ 0] \\ K_2[3p+1,\ 1+p,\ 1+p,\ p-1] \\ K_2[3p+1,\ 1+p,\ 1+p,\ 1-p] \end{matrix}\right\}.$$

It corresponds to the edge

$$K[2, 1, 1, 0]$$

of C_{24}. Their number is 96.

The face

$$F_8[3p+3, 1+p, 1+p, 1+p],$$

is bounded by

$$\left.\begin{array}{l} E_2[1+p, 1-p, p, p] \\ E_2[1+p, p, 1-p, p] \\ E_2[1+p, p, p, 1-p] \end{array}\right\} \text{ and } \left.\begin{array}{l} K_8[2+2p, 2p, 1, 1] \\ K_8[2+2p, 1, 2p, 1] \\ K_8[2+2p, 1, 1, 2p] \end{array}\right\}.$$

It corresponds to the quasi-heterogeneous face

$$F[2, \tfrac{2}{3}, \tfrac{2}{3}, \tfrac{2}{3}]$$

of C_{24}. Their number is 64. Hence the number of triangles is 192.

As the number of K_1 is 96, the number of F_1 is 32 and K_1 appears three times in F_1, we conclude that one F_1 passes through K_1. In the same way we infer that the other edges belong to one triangle.

The first kind of octagon is that, which truncates a quasi-truncated

$$O[1, 1, 1, 1]$$

at the vertex

$$E[2, 2, 0, 0].$$

The faces of O through E are:

$F[\tfrac{4}{3}, \tfrac{4}{3}, \tfrac{4}{3}, 0]$, $F[2, \tfrac{2}{3}, \tfrac{2}{3}, \tfrac{2}{3}]$, $F[\tfrac{4}{3}, \tfrac{4}{3}, 0, \tfrac{4}{3}]$, $F[\tfrac{2}{3}, 2, \tfrac{2}{3}, \tfrac{2}{3}]$

The octagon is limited by the two vertices in these faces, which are nearest to E[2, 2, 0, 0] namely:

$$\begin{array}{ll} E_1[2p, 1, 1, 0], & E_1[1, 2p, 1, 0], \\ E_2[p, 1+p, p, 1-p], & E_2[p, 1+p, 1-p, p], \\ E_1[1, 2p, 0, 1], & E_1[2p, 1, 0, 1], \\ E_2[1+p, p, 1-p, p], & E_2[1+p, p, p, 1-p]. \end{array}$$

This octagon will be represented by

$$F_4[2p+1, 2p+1, 1, 1].$$

The second kind of octagon is that, which truncates a quasi-truncating

$$O[2, 0, 0, 0]$$

at a vertex

$$E[2, 2, 0, 0].$$

Its vertices are

$E_2[1+p, p, p, 1-p]$, $E_2[1+p, p, 1-p, p]$,
$E_2[1+p, p, p-1, p]$, $E_2[1+p, p, -p, 1-p]$,
$E_2[1+p, p, -p, p-1]$, $E_2[1+p, p, p-1, -p]$,
$E_2[1+p, p, 1-p, -p]$, $E_2[1+p, p, p, p-1]$,

and it is represented by

$$F_5[2p+2, 2p, 0, 0].$$

The number of octagons is $96+48=144$. Hence $F=144+192=336$.

There are three notations for the bounding spaces. A quasi-truncated

$$O[1, 1, 1, 1]$$

is transformed into

$$tC_1[1, 1, 1, 1].$$

The vertices of this O are

$E[2, 2, 0, 0]$, $E[2, 0, 2, 0]$, $E[0, 2, 2, 0]$,
$E[0, 0, 2, 2]$, $E[0, 2, 0, 2]$, $E[2, 0, 0, 2]$.

So we have, corresponding to them, the following octagons

$F_4[2p+1, 2p+1, 1, 1]$, $F_4[2p+1, 1, 2p+1, 1]$,
$F_4[1, 2p+1, 2p+1, 1]$, $F_4[1, 1, 2p+1, 2p+1]$,
$F_4[1, 2p+1, 1, 2p+1]$, $F_4[2p+1, 1, 1, 2p+1]$.

The triangles correspond to those which bound the O and which are given page 19. So we have

$F_1[2p+2, 2p+2, 2p+2, 0]$, $F_3[p+1, p+1, p+1, 3p+3]$,
$F_1[2p+2, 2p+2, 0, 2p+2]$, $F_3[p+1, p+1, 3p+3, p+1]$,
$F_1[2p+2, 0, 2p+2, 2p+2]$, $F_3[p+1, 3p+3, p+1, p+1]$,
$F_1[0, 2p+2, 2p+2, 2p+2]$, $F_3[3p+3, p+1, p+1, p+1]$.

The tC corresponding to the quasi-truncating $O[2, 0, 0, 0]$ and which will be represented by

$$tC_2[2, 0, 0, 0]$$

is bounded by the octagons

$F_5[2p+2, \quad 2p,0,0]$, $F_5[2p+2,0, \quad 2p,0]$, $F_5[2p+2,0,0, \quad 2]$,
$F_5[2p+2,-2p,0,0]$, $F_5[2p+2,0,-2p,0]$, $F_5[2p+2,0,0,-2]$,
and by the triangles

$F_3[3p+3, p+1, \quad p+1, \quad p+1]$, $F_3[3p+3, -(p+1), -(p+1), \quad (p+1)]$,
$F_3[3p+3, p+1, -(p+1), \quad p+1]$, $F_3[3p+3, -(p+1), \quad p+1, -(p+1)]$,
$F_3[3p+3, p+1, -(p+1), -(p+1)]$, $F_3[3p+3, -(p+1), \quad p+1, \quad p+1]$,
$F_3[3p+3, p+1, -(p+1), -(p+1)]$, $F_3[3p+3, -(p+1), -(p+1), \quad p+1]$.

The truncating tC at the vertices E[2, 2, 0, 0] will be represented by

$$tC_3[2, 2, 0, 0].$$

In order to determine its faces we have to find the edges and O through E[2, 2, 0, 0]. To the former correspond the triangles; to the latter the octagons. The result is:

$F_5[2p+2, \quad 2p, \quad 0, \quad 0]$, $F_4[2p+1, 2p+1, \quad 1, 1]$,
$F_4[2p+1, 2p+1, \quad 1, -1]$, $F_5[\quad 2p, 2p+2, \quad 0, 0]$,
$F_4[2p+1, 2p+1, -1, -1]$, $F_4[2p+1, 2p+1, -1, 1]$

and

$F_2[4p+2, 2p+1, \quad 2p+1, \quad 0]$, $F_2[2p+1, 4p+2, -(2p+1), \quad 0]$,
$F_2[2p+1, 4p+2, \quad 0, -(2p+1)]$, $F_2[4p+2, 2p+1, \quad 0, \quad 2p+1]$,
$F_2[2p+1, 4p+2, \quad 0, \quad 2p+1]$, $F_2[4p+2, 2p+1, \quad 0, -(2p+1)]$,
$F_2[4p+2, 2p+1, -(2p+1), \quad 0]$, $F_2[2p+1, 4p+2, \quad 2p+1, \quad 0]$.

We will compare the faces and find that through the triangles

$F_1[2p+2, 2p+2, 2p+2, \quad 0]$ pass $tC_1[1, 1, 1, 1]$ and $tC_1[1, 1, 1, -1]$,
$F_2[4p+2, 2p+1, 2p+1, \quad 0]$ „ $tC_3[2, 2, 0, 0]$ „ $tC_3[2, 0, 2, 0]$,
$F_3[3p+3, 1+p, 1+p, 1+p]$ „ $tC_1[1, 1, 1, 1]$ „ $tC_2[2, 0, 0, 0]$,

and through the octagons

$F_4[2p+1, 2p+1, 1, 1]$ pass $tC_1[1, 1, 1, 1]$ „ $tC_3[2, 2, 0, 0]$,
$F_5[2p+2, \quad 2p, 0, 0]$ „ $tC_2[2, 0, 0, 0]$ „ $tC_3[2, 2, 0, 0]$.

The dihedral angle between spaces at a triangle is different from that at an octagon as that angle depends on the face which the two spaces have in common. Thus the faces are totally unequal.

We stated that through an edge passes one triangle. Moreover, through

$K_1[2p+1, 2p+1, 2, 0]$	pass	$F_4[2p+1, 2p+1, 1, 1]$	and	$F_4[2p+1, 2p+1, 1, -1]$,
$K_2[3p+1, p+1, p+1, 1-p]$	„	$F_5[2p+1, 2p+1, 1, 1]$	„	$F_5[2p+1, 1, 2p+1, 1]$,
$K_3[2p+2, 1, 1, 2p]$	„	$F_5[2p+2, 0, 0, 2p]$	„	$F_4[2p+1, 1, 1, 2p+1]$,
$K_4[2p+2, 0, 2p, 2p]$	„	$F_5[2p+2, 0, 0, 2p]$	„	$F_4[2p+2, 0, 2p, 0]$.

This list has been composed with the aid of the list giving the vertices of a given edge and the list giving the vertices of a given octagon.

We conclude that the edges are equal. They are isosceles.

The polytope has two *consecutive* characteristics of regularity. *Its degree of regularity is* $\frac{1}{2}$.

(20, 60, 70, 30). § 24. In case III the vertex polyhedron is a 3-angular antiprism, whose lateral edges are $\sqrt{2}$, those of the bases 1 (1 = edge of polytope). Through a vertex pass $2T + 6P_3$. The two T have only one vertex in common.

We can derive the polytope from C_5 by means of the following construction. Let O_1, O_2, O_3, O_4 and O_5 be the vertices of a C_5. In each bounding T we place a smaller and concentric T, similarly placed. The vertices of the T placed in $O_1 O_2 O_4 O_5$ will be denoted by $C_1 C_2 C_4 C_5$, where the (third) letter C corresponds to the missing index 3, while the indices correspond to those of the nearest vertex of C_5. This T will be denoted T_C. The number of vertices is 20.

At the same time we get five T near the vertices of C_5, e. g. $A_2 C_2 D_2 E_2$ near O_2. This T will be represented by T_2. Let x stand for $O_2 C_2$, then

$$\overline{A_2 C_2} = \frac{1}{6} x \sqrt{6}.$$

The radius of the circumscribed sphere of $T_C = \frac{1}{4} C_1 C_2 \sqrt{6}$.

On the other hand, this radius = that of $C_5 - \overline{O_2 C_2}$

$$\text{or,} \quad " \quad " \quad = \frac{1}{4}\sqrt{6} - x,$$

(where 1 = edge of C_5), whence

$$\overline{C_1 C_2} = 1 - \frac{2}{3} x\sqrt{6}.$$

Now by making

$$\frac{1}{6} x\sqrt{6} = 1 - \frac{2}{3} x\sqrt{6},$$

we find

$$x = \frac{1}{5}\sqrt{6},$$

i. e. the two kinds of T are equal.

These T bound the polytope, but they do not fill the space, as each of them has only one vertex in common with one of the other kind. Through each vertex pass 6 edges, so we have to expect no other.

We find the other limiting spaces by remarking that to any face of C_5 e. g. $O_2 O_4 O_5$ correspond two similarly placed faces $A_2 A_4 A_5$ and $C_2 C_4 C_5$ forming the bases of a P_3. This P_3 will be denoted by

$$P_{AC}.$$

There are 10 such prisms.

The lateral faces of these prisms are yet uncovered. For instance $A_2 C_2 A_4 C_4$ does not belong to an other prism of this kind. But we have besides 10 other P_3. For near the edge $O_2 O_5$ of C_5 we have three parallel edges $A_2 A_5$, $C_2 C_5$, $D_2 D_5$ of the polytope. These are the lateral edges of a P_3 which will be represented by

$$P_{25}.$$

There are 10 such prisms.

The lateral spaces of the P_3 of the first kind are now covered. Those of P_{AC} belong to P_{24}, P_{25} and P_{45}. Inversely those of P_{25} belong to P_{AC}, P_{AD} and P_{CD}. But we must remark that in the face $A_2 C_2 A_4 C_4$ the edge $A_2 C_2$ is lateral edge of P_{AC}, whilst it belongs to the base of P_{25}.

Now the faces of T_2 are also covered. They bound the prisms P_{25}, P_{24}, P_{23} and P_{12}.

It appears that the squares are homogeneous faces, the triangles heterogeneous ones.

The edges are equal. There are two notations: one with equal letters, the other with equal indices.

Through $C_4 C_5$ pass T_C, P_{AC}, P_{45}, P_{BC},
" $C_2 A_2$ " T_2, P_{24}, P_{AC}, P_{25}.

The dihedral angles of prisms appear at an edge of the polytope in the order

$$90°, \ 60°, \ 90°$$

The edge polygon is an isosceles trapezium, one of the bases being $= 1$, the other sides $= \sqrt{2}$ ($1 =$ edge of polytope).

The degree of regularity of the polytope is $\frac{1}{2}$.

4, 576, 672, o). § 25. In case IV the vertex polyhedron is a 4-angular antiprism, the edges of the bases being $= 1$, the lateral edges $= \sqrt{2}$ ($1 =$ edge of polytope).

If we apply to C_{24} an operation analogous to that of the preceding art. we get 24 O in the spaces, and as many at the vertices of C_{24}. By an analogous calculation we find that by making ($1 =$ edge of C_{24})

$$x = \sqrt{2} - 1,$$

(where x represents again the distance of a vertex of the polytope from the nearest vertex of C_{24}), the two kinds of O are equal. Their edges are $(\sqrt{2} - 1)$ times the edge of C_{24}.

Now we have two notations for the vertices:

$E_1[1, \ 1, 2p-1, 2p-1]$ in the quasi-truncated $O[1,1,1,1]$ near $E[2,2,0,0]$,
$E_2[2p, 2-2p, \ 0, \ 0]$ " " " truncating $O[2,0,0,0]$ " $E[2,2,0,0]$.

Now we are able to determine the O:

$O_1[1, 1, 1, 1]$ in the quasi-truncated $O[1, 1, 1, 1]$ is bounded by

$E_1[1, 1, 2p-1, 2p-1]$,

$E_1[1, 2p-1, 1, 2p-1]$, $E_1[1, 2p-1, 2p-1, 1]$, $E_1[2p-1, 1, 2p-1, 1]$, $E_1[2p-1, 1, 1, 2p-1]$,

$E_1[2p-1, 2p-1, 1, 1]$.

$O_2[2, 0, 0, 0]$ in the quasi-truncated $O[2, 0, 0, 0]$ is bounded by

$E_2[2p, 2-2p, 0, 0]$,

$E_2[2p, 0, 2-2p, 0]$, $E_2[2p, 0, 0, 2p-2]$, $E_2[2p, 0, 2p-2, 0]$, $E_2[2p, 0, 0, 2-2p]$,

$E_2[2p, 2p-2, 0, 0]$.

$O_3[2, 2, 0, 0]$ near $E[2, 2, 0, 0]$ is bounded by

$E_2[2p, 2-2p, 0, 0]$,

$E_1[1, 1, 2p-1, 2p-1]$, $E_1[1, 1, 2p-1, 1-2p]$, $E_1[1, 1, 1-2p, 1-2p]$, $E_1[1, 1, 1-2p, 2p-1]$,

$E_2[2-2p, 2p, 0, 0]$.

The number of O is 48.

From this we deduce the four notations for the edges:

$K_1[2, 2p, 2p, 4p-2]$ joins $E_1[1, 1, 2p-1, 2p-1]$ and $E_1[1, 2p-1, 1, 2p-1]$, and is parallel to $K[2, 1, 1, 0]$ in $O[1, 1, 1, 1]$.

$K_2[4p, 2-2p, 2-2p, 0]$ joins $E_2[2p, 2-2p, 0, 0]$ and $E_2[2p, 0, 2-2p, 0]$, and is parallel to $K[2, 1, 1, 0]$ in $O[2, 0, 0, 0]$.

$K_3[2, 2, 4p-2, 0]$ joins $E_1[1, 1, 2p-1, 2p-1]$ and $E_1[1, 1, 2p-1, 1-2p]$.

$K_4[2p+1, 3-2p, 2p-1, 2p-1]$ joins $E_2[2p, 2-2p, 0, 0]$ and $E_1[1, 1, 2p-1, 2p-1]$.

The faces of these O are:

$F_1[3, 4p-1, 4p-1, 4p-1]$ situated in $O[1, 1, 1, 1]$ near the quasi-heterogeneous $F\left[2, \frac{2}{3}, \frac{2}{3}, \frac{2}{3}\right]$ of C_{24},

$F_2[2p+1, 2p+1, 6p-3, 2p+1]$ situated in $O[1, 1, 1, 1]$ near the homogeneous $F\left[\frac{4}{3}, \frac{4}{3}, 0, \frac{4}{3}\right]$ of C_{24},

$F_3[6p, 2-2p, 2-2p, 2-2p]$ situated in $O[2, 0, 0, 0]$ near the quasi-heterogeneous $F\left[2, \frac{2}{3}, \frac{2}{3}, \frac{2}{3}\right]$ of C_{24},

$F_4[2p+2, 4-2p, 4p-2, 0]$ being a face of $O_3[2, 2, 0, 0]$ whose vertices are situated in $O[2, 2, 0, 0]$, $O[1, 1, 1, 1]$ and $O[1, 1, 1, -1]$ of C_{24}.

Thus the number of triangles is 384.

We will now determine the P_8 and at the same time we

will obtain the squares F_5 and F_6. We will discern the P_3 by means of accents. The

$$P'_3[4p+4,\ 2p+2,\ 2p+2,\ 0],$$

to the number of 96, have their lateral edges parallel to

$$K[2,\ 1,\ 1,\ 0]$$

and correspond to the P, having two letter-indices, of case III.

The vertices are

$E_1[1,\ 1, 2p-1, 2p-1]$, $E_1[1,\ 1, 2p-1,\ 1-2p]$, $E_2[2p, 2-2p,\ 0, 0]$,
$E_1[1, 2p-1,\ 1, 2p-1]$, $E_1[1, 2p-1,\ 1,\ 1-2p]$, $E_2[2p,\ 0, 2-2p, 0]$,

and the faces

$$F_4[2p+2,\ 4-2p,\ 4p-2, 0],$$
$$F_6[4p+2, 2, 2, 2-4p],\ F_6[4p+2, 2, 2, 4p-2],\ F_5[4, 4p, 4p, 0],$$
$$F_4[2p+2,\ 4p-2,\ 4-2p, 0].$$

The second kind

$$P''_3[6p+3,\ 2p+1,\ 2p+1,\ 2p+1],$$

to the number of 64, have their bases parallel to

$$F\left[2, \frac{2}{3}, \frac{2}{3}, \frac{2}{3}\right].$$

The vertices and faces are

$E_1[1,\ 1, 2p-1, 2p-1]$, $E_1[1, 2p-1,\ 1, 2p-1]$, $E_1[1, 2p-1, 2p-1,\ 1]$,
$E_2[2p, 2-2p,\ 0,\ 0]$, $E_2[2p,\ 0, 2-2p,\ 0]$, $E_2[2p,\ 0,\ 0, 2-2p]$.

$$F_1[3, 4p-1, 4p-1, 4p-1],$$
$$F_6[4p+2, 4p-2, 2, 2],\ F_6[4p+2, 2, 4p-2, 2],\ F_6[4p+2, 2, 2, 4p-2],$$
$$F_3[6p, 2-2p, 2-2p, 2-2p].$$

The third kind

$$P'''_3[4p+2, 4p+2, 4p+2, 0],$$

to the number of 32, have their bases parallel to

$$F\left[\frac{4}{3}, \frac{4}{3}, \frac{4}{3}, 0\right].$$

The vertices and faces are

$E_1[2p-1, 1, 1, 2p-1]$, $E_1[1, 2p-1, 1, 2p-1]$, $E_1[1, 1, 2p-1, 2p-1]$,
$E_1[2p-1, 1, 1, 1-2p]$, $E_1[1, 2p-1, 1, 1-2p]$, $E_1[1, 1, 2p-1, 1-2p]$.

$$F_2[2p+1,\ 2p+1,\ 2p+1,\ 6p-3],$$
$$F_5[4,\ 4p,\ 4p,\ 0],\ F_5[4p,\ 4,\ 4p,\ 0],\ F_5[4p,\ 4p,\ 4,\ 0],$$
$$F_2[2p+1,\ 2p+1,\ 2p+1,\ 3-6p].$$

The P''_3 and P'''_3 correspond to the P_3 with two letter-indices of case III.

We will now compare the faces.

Through $F_1[3, 4p-1, 4p-1, 4p-1]$ pass $P''_3[6p+3, 2p+1, 2p+1, 2p+1]$ and $O_1[1, 1, 1, 1]$,
„ $F_2[2p+1, 2p+1, 2p+1, 6p-3]$ „ $P'''_3[4p+2, 4p+2, 4p+2, 0]$ „ $O_1[1, 1, 1, 1]$,
„ $F_3[6p, 2-2p, 2-2p, 2-2p]$ „ $P''_3[6p+3, 2p+1, 2p+1, 2p+1]$ „ $O_2[2, 0, 0, 0]$,
„ $F_4[2p+2, 4-2p, 4p-2, 0]$ „ $P'_3[4p+4, 2p+2, 2p+2, 0]$ „ $O_3[2, 2, 0, 0]$,
„ $F_5[4, 4p, 4p, 0]$ „ $P'_3[4p+4, 2p+2, 2p+2, 0]$
and $P'''_3[4p+2, 4p+2, 4p+2, 0]$,
„ $F_6[4p+2, 4p-2, 2, 2]$ „ $P'_3[4p+4, 0, 2p+2, 2p+2]$
and $P''[6p+3, 2p+1, 2p+1, 2p+1]$.

Hence the squares are homogeneous, the triangles heterogeneous.

We will now compare the edges.

Through

$$K_1[2, 2p, 2p, 4p-2]$$

pass

$F_1[3, 4p-1, 4p-1, 4p-1]$, $F_2[2p+1, 2p+1, 2p+1, 6p-3]$, $F_5[4, 4p, 4p, 0]$, $F_6[4p+2, 2, 2, 4p-2]$.

Through

$$K_2[4p, 2-2p, 2-2p, 0]$$

pass

$F_3[6p, 2-2p, 2-2p, 2p-2]$, $F_3[6p, 2-2p, 2-2p, 2-2p]$, $F_6[4p+2, 2, 2, 4p-2]$, $F_6[4p+2, 2, 2, 2-4p]$.

Through

$$K_3[2, 2, 4p-2, 0]$$

pass

$F_4[4-2p, 2p+2, 4p-2, 0]$, $F_4[2p+2, 4-2p, 4p-2, 0]$, $F_5[4, 4p, 4p, 0]$, $F_5[4p, 4, 4p, 0]$.

Through

$$K_4[2p+1, 3-2p, 2p-1, 2p-1]$$

pass

$F_4[2p+2, 4-2p, 0, 4p-2]$, $F_4[2p+2, 4-2p, 4p-2, 0]$, $F_6[4p+2, 2, 2, 4p-2]$, $F_6[4p+2, 2, 4p-2, 2]$.

Hence the edges are equal, and the order of the faces through an edge is: triangle, triangle, square, square.

Hence the order of the angles of P_3 is

$$90°, \ 60°, \ 90°.$$

The edge polygon is an isosceles trapezium, one of the bases being $=1$, the other sides $=\sqrt{2}$ ($1=$ edge of polytope).

The degree of regularity of the polytope is $\frac{1}{2}$.

(n^2, $2n^2$, n^2+2n, $2n$). § 26. In case V four P_n pass through a vertex. The vertex polyhedron is a tetrahedron, two opposite edges of which are equal to the smallest diagonal of a regular polygon of n sides, the other edges $=\sqrt{2}$ ($1=$ edge of polytope). We find

$$K=2E,\ F=\frac{2}{n}E+E,\ R=\frac{2E}{n}.$$

In order to find the absolute value of E, K, F and R we endeavour to build up the polytope for a special case, $n=5$.

We begin by placing four P_5 round a vertex A, as shown in fig. 3. They are AH, AU, AR and AN. The vertices

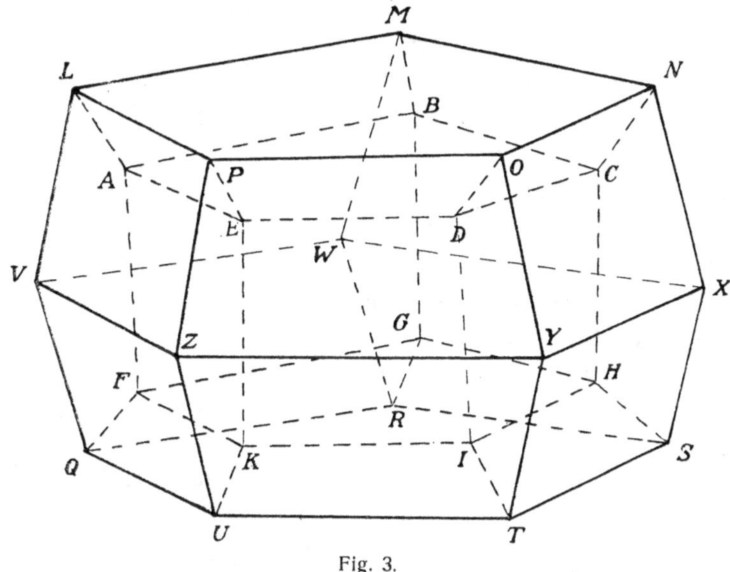

Fig. 3.

B, E, F and L of the vertex polyhedron of A may be considered as the vertices of the spherical tetrahedron which corresponds to the solid angle at A. The edges of that tetrahedron are:

$$LB = BF = FE = EL = 90°, \quad BE = LF = 108°.$$

Hence the angles between great circles are

$$FBE = FEB = BFL = BLF = ELF = EFL = LEB = LBE = 90°,$$
$$BFE = LBF = BLE = LEF = 108°.$$

The angles between great spheres are

$$E . LB . F = E . BF . L = B . FE . L = B . EL . F = 90°,$$
$$F . BE . L = B . LF . E = 108°.$$

Now we get at E four edges which determine a spherical tetrahedron PADK, whose edges are

$$KA = AP = PD = DK = 90°, \qquad KP = AD = 108°$$

and which is consequently equal to that mentioned higher up. Thus we have:

$$DPK = 90°, \quad PKD = 90°, \quad PDK = 108°$$

and, hence, the corresponding angles between faces:

$$D . EP . K = 90°, \quad P . EK . D = 90°, \quad K . ED . P = 108°.$$

Hence it is possible to cover the faces PD, PK, and KD by means of an other prism PT. Proceeding in this way we can enclose the prism AH in 5 prisms. But then we get at the same time the prisms VN, QX and QH. Now we find that through each face pass two prisms and that the polytope is closed.

It is obvious that this demonstration holds for the general case, and that we get

$$E = n^2, \quad K = 2n^2, \quad F = n^2 + 2n, \quad R = 2n.$$

So we have an infinite number of polytopes which are called *prismotopes*.

The spaces are equal but, notwithstanding, we will divide them into two kinds of n prisms each, so that two of the same kind have a polygon of n sides in common, and two of different kinds a square.

The $2n$ polygons of n sides may be divided into two kinds, each of n polygons. Those of the same kind are parallel to each other and perfectly perpendicular to those of the other kind. The former property is obvious. In order to prove the latter we have but to remark that

$$PO \perp PE, \quad PO \perp PZ, \quad LP \perp PE, \quad LP \perp PZ.$$

From these properties we deduce a simple way of describing the polytope. In two planes perfectly perpendicular to each other we draw equal regular polygons of n sides. The vertices of these polygons are the projections of the vertices of the polytope.

These polygons will be called the *auxiliary* polygons. We can consider the planes $OX_1 X_2$ and $OX_3 X_4$ of a rectangular system of coordinates $O(X_1 X_2 X_3 X_4)$ as the perfectly perpendicular planes and in these planes draw the auxiliary polygons round O, which is to become the centre of the polytope, as a centre, in such a position that OX_1 and OX_3 pass through vertices.

The coordinates of the vertices of the polytope with respect to the described system are in terms of the edge

$$\cos\frac{2\pi l}{n},\ \sin\frac{2\pi l}{n},\ \cos\frac{2\pi m}{n},\ \sin\frac{2\pi m}{n},$$

$$(l = 1, 2, \ldots n),$$
$$(m = 1, 2, \ldots n).$$

We will represent a vertex by

$$E(l, m),$$

where l refers to x_1 and x_2, m to x_3 and x_4.

The edge through $E(l, m)$ and $E(l, m+1)$ has for midpoint

$$\cos\frac{2\pi l}{n},\ \sin\frac{2\pi l}{n},\ \sin\frac{\pi}{n}\cos\frac{2\pi(m+\frac{1}{2})}{n},\ \sin\frac{\pi}{n}\sin\frac{2\pi(m+\frac{1}{2})}{n}.$$

We will represent that edge by

$$K(l, m+\tfrac{1}{2}).$$

It is perpendicular to $OX_1 X_2$ and parallel to $OX_3 X_4$. Inversely $K(l+\frac{1}{2}, m)$ is perpendicular to $OX_3 X_4$ and parallel to $OX_1 X_2$.

A polygon of n sides parallel to OX_3X_4 and perpendicular to OX_1X_2 has for centre

$$\cos\frac{2\pi l}{m},\ \sin\frac{2\pi l}{n},\ 0,\ 0.$$

We will represent it by

$$p_n(l,\ 0).$$

It is bounded by

$$E(l,\quad m),\quad (m=1,\dots n),$$
$$\text{and } K(l,\ m+\tfrac{1}{2}),\quad (m=1,\dots n).$$

Inversely $p_n(0,\ m)$ is parallel to OX_1X_2 and perpendicular to OX_3X_4.

In a square two adjacent sides belong to different kinds of p_n. Its projection on OX_1X_2 and OX_3X_4 is a side of an auxiliary polygon. We will represent one of these squares by

$$p_4(l+\tfrac{1}{2},\ m+\tfrac{1}{2}).$$

It has for vertices and edges

$$\left.\begin{matrix} E(l,\ m+1) \\ E(l,\ m) \\ E(l+1,\ m+1) \\ E(l+1,\ m) \end{matrix}\right\},\quad \left.\begin{matrix} K(l+\tfrac{1}{2},\ m) \\ K(l,\ m+\tfrac{1}{2}) \\ K(l+\tfrac{1}{2},\ m+1) \\ K(l+1,\ m+\tfrac{1}{2}) \end{matrix}\right\}.$$

The projection of a P_n of the first kind on OX_3X_4 is the auxiliary polygon, on OX_1X_2 a side of the auxiliary polygon. Thus we may represent one of them by

$$P_n(l+\tfrac{1}{2},\ 0).$$

It is bounded by

$$\left.\begin{matrix} E(l,\ m) \\ \\ E(l+1,\ m) \end{matrix}\right\},\quad \left.\begin{matrix} K(l,\ m+\tfrac{1}{2}) \\ K(l+\tfrac{1}{2},\ m) \\ K(l+1,\ m+\tfrac{1}{2}) \\ (m=1,2,\dots n) \end{matrix}\right\},\quad \left.\begin{matrix} p_n(l,\ 0) \\ p_4(l+\tfrac{1}{2},\ m+\tfrac{1}{2}) \\ p_n(l+1,\ 0) \end{matrix}\right\}.$$

The projection of a P_n of the other kind

$$P_n(0,\ m+\tfrac{1}{2})$$

on OX_1X_2 is the auxiliary polygon, on OX_3X_4 a side of the auxiliary polygon.

We will now compare the faces. Through

$$p_n(l,\ 0)$$

pass

$$P_n(l+\tfrac{1}{2},\ 0) \quad \text{and} \quad P_n(l-\tfrac{1}{2},\ 0).$$

Through

$$p_4(1+\tfrac{1}{2},\ m+\tfrac{1}{2})$$

pass

$$P_n(l+\tfrac{1}{2},\ 0) \quad \text{and} \quad P_n(0,\ m+\tfrac{1}{2}).$$

Hence two similarly indicated P_n have a p_n in common, two differently indicated a p_4. So these two kinds of P_n are those mentioned on page 58.

The edges are isosceles. Through

$$K(l,\ m+\tfrac{1}{2})$$

pass

$$p_4(l+\tfrac{1}{2},\ m+\tfrac{1}{2}),\ p_4(l-\tfrac{1}{2},\ m+\tfrac{1}{2}),\ p_n(l,\ 0).$$

Through

$$K(l+\tfrac{1}{2},\ m)$$

pass

$$p_4(l+\tfrac{1}{2},\ m+\tfrac{1}{2}),\ \ p_4(l+\tfrac{1}{2},\ m-\tfrac{1}{2}),\ \ p_n(0,\ m).$$

Hence the edges are equal.

The degree of regularity is $\frac{1}{2}$.

CHAPTER IV.

FIVEDIMENSIONAL SEMIREGULAR POLYTOPES.

Regular polytopes in S_n.

§ 27. In a space of n dimensions ($n > 4$) there are only 3 regular polytopes [1]), which we will represent by S_n, Cr_n and M_n.

S_n is the regular simplex.

Cr_n is analogous to C_{16}. We can obtain its vertices by taking on each axis of a rectangular system two points at equal distances from the origin. It is called *cross polytope*.

M_n is analogous to C_8. It is the reciprocal polar of Cr_n and is called *measure polytope*.

Preliminary remarks for S_5.

§ 28. It is obvious how the definitions of "degree of regularity" as given in art. 7 and 10 for S_3 and S_4 are to be extended for S_5. It is our aim to determine the polytopes whose degree of regularity is $\frac{1}{2}$ or more. Hence, as far as those of the first kind are concerned, we have to find polytopes having equal vertices, equal edges and at least half-equal faces. So we have to expect only C_5, C_{16}, C_{24}, C_{600}, tC_5 and tC_{600} among the bounding polytopes.

In the present investigation we will refer occasionally to the following list of angles. The angles in the column "solid angles" are spherical excesses.

The sum of the dihedral angles at a face of a 5-dimensional polytope must be $< 360°$, the sum of the solid angles

---

1) Compare e. g. Dr. P. H. SCHOUTE, *Mehrdimensionale Geometrie*, II, 244.

	Dihedral angles between polyhedra	Solid angles round an edge
C_5	75° 31′ 21″	46° 34′ 3″
C_{16}	120°	120°
C_{24}	120°	180°
C_{600}	164° 28′ 39″	282° 23′ 15″
tC_5	(O, O) = 75° 31′ 21″, (T, O) = 104° 28′ 39″	104° 28′ 39″
tC_{600}	(O, O) = 164° 28′ 39″, (O, I) = 157° 41′ 12″	299° 51′ 3″

at an edge must be $<$ 720°.

By what has been said in art. 10 it will be clear what is meant by the terms "*vertex polytope*", "*edge polyhedron*" and "*face polygon*".

The number of the bounding elements of a 5-dimensional polytope will be indicated by r_0, r_1, r_2, r_3 and r_4; they are connected by the extended EULER's formula [1])

$$r_0 - r_1 + r_2 - r_3 + r_4 = 2.$$

The elements of a vertex polytope will be indicated by E, K, F and R; those of an edge polyhedron by e, k and f.

We will represent the number of edges through a vertex of the polytope by x.

The length of the edge will be taken as unit.

[E]xclusion of [C]$_{600}$ and tC_{600} [a]s bounding [p]olytopes.

§ 29. Before determining the combinations of polytopes we will have to consider, we will show that C_{600} and tC_{600} cannot appear as bounding polytopes.

We infer from the list of angles that C_{600} might be combined with C_5 and tC_5. It cannot appear at a face through which 4 polytopes pass; moreover only a single C_{600} can lie round a face of 3 polytopes, while faces of 5 polytopes must be entirely excluded.

Let us first combine C_{600} with C_5. In the edge polyhedron

1) Ibid. 62.

C_{600} and C_5 are represented respectively by a regular pentagon and a regular triangle whose sides are 1. As the vertices of the edge polyhedron represent the faces of the polytope there can be no vertex of 5 edges; no pentagon can pass through a vertex of 4 edges, and only one through a vertex of 3 edges. Hence the two other faces through any of the vertices of a pentagon are triangles. Hence the polyhedron is necessarily a 5-angular pyramid. But this must be rejected as 5 edges pass through its summit.

The same reasoning holds for the combination of C_{600} and tC_5. Then the lateral edges are $\sqrt{2}$.

For the combination of C_{600}, C_5 and tC_5 it is even impossible to construct an edge polyhedron.

Any tC_{600} must have an I in common with an other. Hence there are two angles (O, I) at the face of such an I. So there is no room for an other angle.

Semiregulars with one kind of bounding cells (C_5 or tC_5). § 30. After having excluded C_{600} and tC_{600} we will now try to find semiregular polytopes with one kind of bounding polytopes. And then it is obvious, as at least 3 polyhedra pass through a face, that we have only to consider C_5 and tC_5.

In the case of C_5 the edge polyhedron is bounded by equilateral triangles only. We cannot admit vertices of 5 edges or more. Thus we have to consider T, a 3-angular bipyramid and O.

T and O lead respectively to the simplex and the cross polytope.

The bipyramid admits no circumscribed sphere. Hence it cannot be edge polyhedron, there being no point without its space which is equidistant from its vertices.

In the case of tC_5 the edge polyhedron is bounded by isosceles triangles $(\sqrt{2}, \sqrt{2}, 1)$. An angle $(\sqrt{2}, \sqrt{2}) = \alpha$ corresponds to the angle (O, O) in tC_5, an angle $(1, \sqrt{2}) = \beta$ to the angle (T, O) of tC_5. We can admit only the following vertices:

a). vertices with the edges $\sqrt{2}, \sqrt{2}, \sqrt{2}$ and the angles α, α, α,
b). „ „ „ „ $\sqrt{2}, \sqrt{2}, 1$ „ „ „ β, β, α,
c). „ „ „ „ $\sqrt{2}, \sqrt{2}, \sqrt{2}, \sqrt{2}$ „ „ „ $\alpha, \alpha, \alpha, \alpha$.

Besides we find

$$e = 2 + \frac{f}{2}, \ k = \frac{3}{2} f.$$

From $f > 8$ would result vertices of 5 edges and more.

For $f = 8$ the polyhedron would have only vertices of 4 edges and consequently there would be no place for the edges 1.

The case $f = 6$ leads to a 3-angular bipyramid. Here again there is no place for the edges 1, as each edge passes through a vertex of 4 edges.

In the case $f = 4$ we can construct the polyhedron. It is a tetrahedron, two opposite edges being $= 1$, the others $= \sqrt{2}$. Its degree of regularity is $\frac{1}{3}$; hence that of the vertex polytope is $\frac{1}{2}$ and that of the polytope is $\frac{3}{5}$.

Thus we get

$$e = 4, \quad k = 2 + 4, \quad f = 4$$

and hence

$$E = x, \quad K = 2x, \quad F = \left(\frac{2}{3} + 1\right) x, \quad R = \frac{2}{3} x.$$

So x must be a multiple of 3. We find for the polytope

$$r_1 = \frac{x r_0}{2}, \ r_2 = \frac{2}{3} x r_0, \ r_3 = \left(\frac{1}{6} + \frac{1}{6}\right) x r_0, \ r_4 = \frac{1}{15} x r_0,$$

whence, by the extended Euler's theorem,

$$r_0 \left(1 - \frac{1}{10} x\right) = 2.$$

Now, as $1 - \frac{1}{10} x$ must be positive, we get

$$x < 10.$$

On the other hand, as the number of vertices of a tC_5 is 10, r_0 must be > 10, whence we deduce

$$x > 8.$$

Hence we have only to consider

$$x = 9,$$

whence

$$E = 9, \quad K = 18, \quad F = 6 + 9, \quad R = 6.$$

This is the prismotope $n = 3$. Now we find in S_5:

$$r_0 = 20, \quad r_1 = 90, \quad r_2 = 120, \quad r_3 = 30 + 30, \quad r_4 = 12.$$

We will prove the existence of this polytope in the pages that follow.

Semiregulars with two kinds of bounding cells.

§ 31. We will now endeavour to determine the semi-regular polytopes bounded by two kinds of cells, and then we have to consider the following combinations:

A. . . . C_5 , C_{16},
B. . . . C_5 , tC_5,
C. . . . C_{16} , tC_5,
D. . . . C_{24} , tC_5.

We need not consider the combinations (C_5, C_{24}) and (C_{16}, C_{24}), the bounding polyhedra being different.

Case **A.** Combination C_5, C_{16}.

Let us suppose that through an edge pass

$$pC_{16} \text{ and } qC_5.$$

In the edge polyhedron a square (1, 1, 1, 1) corresponds to C_{16}, and a triangle (1, 1, 1) to C_5. So

$$e = 2 + p + \frac{q}{2}, \quad k = 2p + \frac{3}{2}q, \quad f = p + q.$$

Hence q must be even.

We might now proceed to try all the values for p and q within the limits resulting from the sum of angles. But beforehand we will simplify the discussion by means of the following remarks.

1°. We infer from the list of angles that we cannot

admit vertices of 5 edges, as a plane angle in the edge polyhedron corresponds to an angle between polyhedra in the polytope. So

$$k \leqq 2e,$$

whence

$$q \leqq 8.$$

2⁰. Then we infer from the list of angles that, if 3 polyhedra pass through a face, at least one of the angles must be $75° \, 31' \, 21''$, and that, in the case of 4 polyhedra through a face, at least three angles must be $75° \, 31' \, 21''$. Thus in the edge polyhedron at a vertex of 3 edges we expect at least one triangle, at a vertex of 4 edges at least 3 triangles.

Let e_3 and e_4 represent respectively the numbers of vertices of 3 and 4 edges, then

$$e_3 = 8 - q,$$

$$e_4 = p + \frac{3}{2} q - 6.$$

The number of bounding triangles is, at least,

$$\frac{e_3 + 3e_4}{3},$$

whence

$$q \geqq p + \frac{7}{6} q - \frac{10}{3},$$

i. e.

$$6p + q \leqq 20.$$

In consequence of these remarks we have to consider only:

$$q = 2 \begin{cases} p = 2 \\ p = 3 \end{cases}, \quad q = 4 \begin{cases} p = 1 \\ p = 2 \end{cases}, \quad q = 6 \begin{cases} p = 1 \\ p = 2 \end{cases}, \quad q = 8 \begin{cases} p = 1 \\ p = 2 \end{cases}.$$

a). The case $q = 2$, $p = 2$ must be rejected, a tetrahedron having no squares.

b). For $q = 2$, $p = 3$ we find

$$e = 6, \quad k = 9, \quad f = 2 + 3,$$

$$E = x, \quad K = 3x, \quad F = (2 + 1)x, \quad R\left(\frac{1}{2} + \frac{1}{2}\right)x.$$

Hence x must be even;

$$r_1 = \frac{xr_0}{2},\ r_2 = xr_0,\ r_3 = \left(\frac{1}{2} + \frac{1}{4}\right)xr_0,\ \ r_4 = \left(\frac{1}{10} + \frac{1}{16}\right)xr$$

whence, by the extended EULER's formula

$$r_0\left(1 - \frac{7}{80}x\right) = 2.$$

By remarking that r_0 must be positive, we get:

$$1 - \frac{7}{80}x > 0,$$
$$x < 12,$$

and by remarking that r_0 must be necessarily > 8, we find

$$\frac{2}{1 - \frac{7}{80}x} > 8,$$
$$x > 8.$$

Hence $x = 10$ and therefore

$$\mathrm{E} = 10,\quad \mathrm{K} = 30,\quad \mathrm{F} = 10 + 5,\quad \mathrm{R} = 5 + 5,$$
$$r_0 = 16,\ r_1 = 80,\ r_2 = 160,\ r_3 = 80 + 40,\ r_4 = 16 + 10.$$

The vertex polytope is tC_5; its degree of regularity is $\frac{2\frac{1}{2}}{4}$.

Consequently that of the polytope is $\frac{3\frac{1}{2}}{5} = \frac{7}{10}$. It is bounded by 16 C_5 and 10 C_{16}, by 120 T. Of the latter 80 are heterogeneous, 40 homogeneous. Its existence will be demonstrated in the following pages.

c). For $q = 4,\ p = 1$ we have
$e = 5,\ k = 4 + 4,\ f = 4 + 1$ (regular 4-angular pyramid),

$$\mathrm{E} = x,\ \ \mathrm{K} = \frac{5}{2}x,\ \ \mathrm{F} = \left(\frac{4}{3} + \frac{4}{3}\right)x,\ \ \mathrm{R} = \left(1 + \frac{1}{6}\right)x,$$

$$r_1 = \frac{xr_0}{2},\ r_2 = \frac{5}{6}xr_0,\ r_3 = \left(\frac{1}{3} + \frac{1}{3}\right)xr_0,\ r_4 = \left(\frac{1}{5} + \frac{1}{48}\right)xr_0,$$

$$r_0\left(1 - \frac{9}{80}x\right) = 2.$$

Hence x must be a multiple of 6. Besides

$$1 - \frac{9}{80}x > 0,$$
$$x < 9.$$

Hence $x = 6$. But this leads to the impossibility $r_0 = \frac{80}{13}$.

d). For $q=4, \ p=2$ we get

$$e=6, \qquad k=10, \qquad f=4+2.$$

The two squares must have an edge in common, else e would be >6. Let AB be the common edge, then A and B are vertices of three edges (faces), and the third faces through A and B are triangles. But so we are led to a 3-angular prism.

e). For $q=6, \ p=1$ we have

$$e=6, \qquad k=11, \qquad f=6+1,$$

$$\mathrm{E}=x, \quad \mathrm{K}=3x, \quad \mathrm{F}=\frac{11}{3}x, \quad \mathrm{R}=\left(\frac{3}{2}+\frac{1}{6}\right)x,$$

$$r_1=\frac{xr_0}{2}, \ r_2=xr_0, \ r_3=\frac{11}{12}xr_0, \ r_4=\left(\frac{3}{10}+\frac{1}{48}\right)xr_0,$$

$$r_0\left(1-\frac{23}{240}x\right)=2.$$

Hence x must be a multiple of 6. Moreover, r_0 being >0, we have

$$1-\frac{23}{240}x>0, \text{ whence } x<11,$$

and r_0 being >8 we have

$$\frac{2}{1-\frac{23}{240}x}>8, \text{ whence } x>7.$$

But x being a multiple of 6 this case must be rejected.

f). For $q=6, \ p=2$ we find

$$e=7, \qquad k=13, \qquad f=6+2,$$

$$e_3=2, \qquad e_4=5.$$

The two squares must have an edge in common. For they must have at least one vertex in common, else we would get $e>7$. But they cannot have only one vertex in common for that would lead to 2 squares through a vertex of 4 edges. Now let AB be the common edge of the squares ABCD and ABEF. The third faces through A and B must be triangles. Hence CE and DF are edges of the polyhedron. Now there are yet one vertex, 4 edges, and 4 triangles wanting.

The wanting vertex is the summit of a 4-angular pyramid whose base is CDEF. So the edge polyhedron consists of a P_3 and a pyramid that have a square in common. But this polyhedron does not admit a circumscribed sphere. Hence there is no point without its space at equal distances from its vertices. So this case must be rejected.

g). For $q=8$, $p=1$ we get

$$e=7, \quad k=14, \quad f=8+1,$$
$$e_3=0, \quad e_4=7.$$

Hence through 4 vertices pass 3 triangles and 1 square; through 3 vertices pass 4 triangles. In order to build up the polyhedron we consider a square and a triangle which have nothing in common. Then the vertices are complete. As to the wanting edges, two pass through any of the vertices, consequently 6 issue from the triangle, 8 from the square. As any of these edges joins a vertex of the square to a vertex of the triangle this case cannot be realized.

h). Finally $q=8$, $p=2$ gives

$$e=8, \quad k=16, \quad f=8+2,$$
$$e_3=0.$$

The squares have nothing in common. This polyhedron is AP_4. Now we demonstrated before (pag. 36) that there is no corresponding cell.

Case **B.** Combination C_5, tC_5.

Let p be the number of C_5, q the number of tC_5 through an edge. Then:

$$e=2+\frac{p}{2}+\frac{q}{2}, \quad k=\frac{3}{2}p+\frac{3}{2}q, \quad f=p+q.$$

In the edge polyhedron C_5 is represented by a triangle (1, 1, 1), tC_5 by a triangle $(\sqrt{2}, \sqrt{2}, 1)$.

An angle $(1, 1)=\alpha$ corresponds to the angle (T, T) of C_5.

" " $(\sqrt{2}, \sqrt{2})=\alpha$ " " " " (O, O) " tC_5.

" " $(1, \sqrt{2})=\beta$ " " " " (T, O) " " .

Hence we can admit the following vertices:

a).	$(1, 1, 1)$	(α, α, α),
b).	$(1, 1, \sqrt{2})$	(α, β, β),
c).	$(1, \sqrt{2}, \sqrt{2})$.	(α, β, β),
d).	$(\sqrt{2}, \sqrt{2}, \sqrt{2})$	(α, α, α),
e).	$(1, 1, 1, 1)$	$(\alpha, \alpha, \alpha, \alpha)$,
f).	$(\sqrt{2}, \sqrt{2}, \sqrt{2}, \sqrt{2})$ . .	$(\alpha, \alpha, \alpha, \alpha)$.

As $p+q$ must be even and as we cannot admit 5 edges through a vertex we have to consider the cases:

1^0. $p+q=8$. There are only vertices of 4 edges. So there would be no place for β.

2^0. $p+q=6$. This is a 3-angular bipyramid. There are 2 vertices of 3 and 3 of 4 edges. But as through any of the latter passes only one kind of edges (see cases *e* and *f*), there would be no place for the other kind.

3^0. $p+q=4$. If we construct a triangle $(\sqrt{2}, \sqrt{2}, 1)$ then the adjacent faces are necessarily equal to it. So there is only one triangle $(1, 1, 1)$ and we find

$$e=1+3, \quad k=3+3, \quad f=1+3,$$

$$E=x, \ K=\left(\frac{1}{2}+\frac{3}{2}\right)x, \ F=\left(1+\frac{3}{4}\right)x, \ R=\left(\frac{1}{4}+\frac{1}{2}\right)x,$$

$$r_1=\frac{xr_0}{2}, \ r_2=\left(\frac{1}{6}+\frac{1}{2}\right)xr_0, \ r_3=\left(\frac{1}{4}+\frac{1}{8}\right)xr_0, \ r_4=\left(\frac{1}{20}+\frac{1}{20}\right)xr_0,$$

whence, by EULER's formula,

$$r_0\left\{1-\frac{13}{120}x\right\}=2.$$

The condition that r_0 must be positive leads to

$$x<10$$

and as x must be a multiple of 4 (and necessarily $\geqq 5$) the only case to be considered is

$$x=8,$$

whence

$$E=8, \quad K=4+12, \quad F=8+6, \quad R=2+4,$$

$$r_0=15, \ r_1=60, \ r_2=20+60, \ r_3=30+15, \ r_4=6+6.$$

The vertex polytope is bounded by 2 T and 4 P_8, by 8 triangles and 6 squares. The vertices are equal; the edges have equal lengths but through 4 of them pass 3 squares (and 3 P_8) while through the 12 other pass 2 triangles and 1 square (2 P_8 and 1 T). It is a regular prism whose bases are T; we denote it by P_T. It shows $1\frac{1}{2}$ characteristics of regularity.

The polytope is bounded by 6 C_5 and 6 tC_5, by 30 T and 15 O. The vertices and edges are equal. The faces are equal triangles, but 20 among them belong to 3 O (and 3 tC_5), the 60 other to 2 T and 1 O (2 tC_5 and 1 C_5). It shows $2\frac{1}{2}$ characteristics of regularity.

Its existence will be demonstrated further on.

Case **C.** Combination C_{16}, tC_5.

Let p be the number of C_{16}, q the number of tC_5 through an edge; then the edge polyhedron is limited by p squares (1, 1, 1, 1) and q triangles ($\sqrt{2}$, $\sqrt{2}$, 1).

The angle $(\sqrt{2}, \sqrt{2}) = \alpha$ corresponds to the angle (O, O) of tC_5,
" " $(1, 1) = \beta$ " " " " (T, O) " " ,
" " $(1, 1) = \gamma$ " " " " (T, T) " C_{16}.

We can admit the following vertices:

a). $(\sqrt{2}, \sqrt{2}, \sqrt{2})$ . . . . . (α, α, α),
b). $(1, \sqrt{2}, \sqrt{2})$ . . . . . . (α, β, β),
c). $(1, 1, \sqrt{2})$ . . . . (β, β, γ),
d). $(\sqrt{2}, \sqrt{2}, \sqrt{2}, \sqrt{2})$ . . $(\beta, \beta, \beta, \beta)$.

Let us consider a bounding square. We infer from this list that through its vertices pass 3 edges (case *c*); that the third edge through any of its vertices is $\sqrt{2}$ and that, consequently, its adjacent faces are triangles. Hence the edge polyhedron is a regular 4-angular pyramid whose lateral edges are $\sqrt{2}$. Hence

$$e = 1 + 4, \quad k = 4 + 4, \quad f = 1 + 4,$$

$$E = x, \quad K = \left(\frac{1}{2} + 2\right)x, \quad F = \left(\frac{4}{3} + 1\right)x, \quad R = \left(\frac{1}{6} + \frac{2}{3}\right)x,$$

$$r_1 = \frac{xr_0}{2}, \quad r_2 = \left(\frac{1}{6} + \frac{2}{3}\right)xr_0, \quad r_3 = \left(\frac{1}{3} + \frac{1}{6}\right)xr_0, \quad r_4 = \left(\frac{1}{48} + \frac{1}{15}\right)xr_0$$

whence by EULER's formula

$$r_0\left(1 - \frac{19}{240}x\right) = 2.$$

The condition that r_0 must be positive leads to

$$x < 13.$$

As x must be a multiple of 6 and cannot be 6, (for one P_3 bounding the vertex polytope has 6 vertices) we have to consider only

$$x = 12,$$

whence

$$E = 12, \quad K = 6 + 24, \quad F = 16 + 12, \quad R = 2 + 8,$$

$$r_0 = 40, \; r_1 = 240, \; r_2 = 80 + 320, \; r_3 = 160 + 80, \; r_4 = 10 + 32.$$

The vertex polytope is bounded by 2 O and 8 P_3, by 16 triangles and 12 squares. Its vertices are equal. Among its edges there are 6, through which pass 4 squares (and 4 P_3), whilst through any of the 24 other edges pass 2 triangles and 1 square (two P_3 and 1 O). It is a prism P_0 whose bases are O. Its degree of regularity is $\frac{3}{8}$.

The polytope itself is bounded by 10 C_{16} and 32 tC_5, by 160 T and 80 O. Its vertices and edges are equal. The faces are equal triangles. But through 80 faces pass 4 O (4 tC_5); through the other 320 pass 2T and 1O (2 tC_5 and 1 C_{16}). Thus it shows $2\frac{1}{2}$ characteristics of regularity.

Its existence will be demonstrated further on.

Case **D**. Combination C_{24}, tC_5.

Let p be the number of C_{24}, q the number of tC_5 through an edge; then the edge polyhedron is bounded by p triangles $(\sqrt{2}, \sqrt{2}, \sqrt{2})$ and q triangles $(\sqrt{2}, \sqrt{2}, 1)$.

The angle $(\sqrt{2}, \sqrt{2}) = \alpha$ in $\triangle(\sqrt{2}, \sqrt{2}, 1)$ corresponds to (O, O) in tC_5.

The angle $(1, \sqrt{2}) = \beta$ in $\triangle(\sqrt{2}, \sqrt{2}, 1)$ corresponds to (T, O) in tC_5.

The angle $(\sqrt{2}, \sqrt{2}) = \gamma$ in $\triangle(\sqrt{2}, \sqrt{2}, \sqrt{2})$ corresponds to (O, O) in C_{24}.

We can admit the following vertices:

a). $(\sqrt{2}, \sqrt{2}, \sqrt{2})$ . . . . (α, α, α),
b). $(\sqrt{2}, \sqrt{2}, \sqrt{2})$ . . . . (α, α, γ),
c). $(\sqrt{2}, \sqrt{2}, \sqrt{2})$ . . . . (α, γ, γ),
d). $(\sqrt{2}, \sqrt{2}, 1)$ . . . . . (α, β, β),
e). $(\sqrt{2}, \sqrt{2}, 1)$ . . . . . (γ, β, β),
f). $(\sqrt{2}, \sqrt{2}, \sqrt{2}, \sqrt{2})$. . . $(\alpha, \alpha, \alpha, \alpha)$,
g). $(\sqrt{2}, \sqrt{2}, \sqrt{2}, \sqrt{2})$. . . $(\alpha, \alpha, \alpha, \gamma)$.

Let us consider a bounding triangle ABC, of which $AB = BC = \sqrt{2}$ and $AC = 1$. Then we infer from the list that A and C are vertices of 3 edges (cases *d* and *e*). Hence we have to add the edges $AD = CD = \sqrt{2}$. Consequently the polyhedron is a tetrahedron. But we have yet to decide which of the cases *d* and *e* are realized at A and C, in other words whether $BD = 1$ or $= \sqrt{2}$. It is obvious that in the former supposition there would be no triangle $(\sqrt{2}, \sqrt{2}, \sqrt{2})$. Thus the edge polyhedron is limited by 5 edges $\sqrt{2}$ and one edge 1. Hence

$$e = 2 + 2, \quad k = 1 + 5, \quad f = 2 + 2,$$

$$E = x, \quad K = (1 + 1)x, \quad F = \left(\frac{1}{3} + \frac{5}{4}\right)x, \quad R = \left(\frac{1}{4} + \frac{1}{3}\right)x,$$

$$r_1 = \frac{xr_0}{2}, \; r_2 = \left(\frac{1}{3} + \frac{1}{3}\right)xr_0, \; r_3 = \left(\frac{1}{12} + \frac{5}{24}\right)xr_0, \; r_4 = \left(\frac{1}{96} + \frac{1}{30}\right)xr_0,$$

whence by EULER's formula

$$r_0\left(1 - \frac{39}{480}x\right) = 2.$$

The condition that r_0 must be positive leads to

$$x < 13.$$

As x must be a multiple of 3 and 4 we have to consider

$$x = 12.$$

Hence

$$E = 12, \quad K = 12 + 12, \quad F = 4 + 15, \quad R = 3 + 4,$$

$$r_0 = 80, \; r_1 = 480, \; r_2 = 320 + 320, \; r_3 = 80 + 200, \; r_4 = 10 + 32.$$

The vertex polytope is bounded by 3 C and 4 P_3, by 4 triangles and 15 squares. The vertices are equal. Among the edges there are 12 through which pass 3 squares (2 C and 1 P_3); through any of the remaining 12 edges pass 2 squares and 1 triangle (1 C and 2 P_3). It is a prism whose bases are P_3, i. e. a prismotope with a triangle and a square as auxiliary polygons. It shows $1\frac{1}{2}$ characteristics of regularity.

The polytope itself is bounded by 10 C_{24} and 32 tC_5; by 80 T and 200 O. The vertices and edges are equal. Through 320 faces pass 3 O (2 C_{24} and 1 tC_5); through any of the 320 other faces pass 2 O and 1 T (1 C_{24} and 2 tC_5). Its degree of regularity is $\frac{1}{2}$.

It will be shown in the pages that follow that the polytope really exists.

Three kinds of bounding cells.

§ 32. We have to consider the following cases, none of which can be realized:

A) . . . . . C_5, tC_5, C_{16},
B) . . . . . C_5, tC_5, C_{24},
C) . . . . . C_{16}, tC_5, C_{24}.

Case **A**. Combination C_5, tC_5, C_{16}.

The faces which bound the edge polyhedron are:

triangles	(1, 1, 1)	corresponding to C_5,
„	($\sqrt{2}$, $\sqrt{2}$, 1)	„ „ tC_5,
squares	(1, 1, 1, 1)	„ „ C_{16}.

The angle $(1, 1) = \alpha$ in triangle $(1, 1, 1)$ corresponds to (T, T) in C_5.

The angle $(\sqrt{2}, \sqrt{2}) = \alpha$ in triangle $(\sqrt{2}, \sqrt{2}, 1)$ corresponds to (T, O) in tC_5.

The angle $(1, \sqrt{2}) = \beta$ in triangle $(\sqrt{2}, \sqrt{2}, 1)$ corresponds to (T, O) in tC_5.

The angle $(1, 1) = \gamma$ in square $(1, 1, 1, 1)$ corresponds to (T, T) in C_{16}.

We can admit the following vertices:

a).	$(\sqrt{2}, \sqrt{2}, \sqrt{2})$	(α, α, α),
b).	$(1, \sqrt{2}, \sqrt{2})$	(α, β, β),
c).	$(1, 1, \sqrt{2})$	(β, β, α),
d).	$(1, 1, \sqrt{2})$	(β, β, γ),
e).	$(1, 1, 1)$	(α, α, α),
f).	$(1, 1, 1)$	(α, α, γ),
g).	$(1, 1, 1)$	(α, γ, γ),
h).	$(\sqrt{2}, \sqrt{2}, \sqrt{2}, \sqrt{2})$ . . .	$(\alpha, \alpha, \alpha, \alpha)$,
i).	$(1, 1, 1, 1)$	$(\alpha, \alpha, \alpha, \alpha)$,
j).	$(1, 1, 1, 1)$	$(\alpha, \alpha, \alpha, \gamma)$.

We will demonstrate the impossibility of this case. Let us consider a bounding triangle ABC, where $AB = BC = \sqrt{2}$ and $AC = 1$. Then the adjacent faces at AB and BC are necessarily triangles $(\sqrt{2}, \sqrt{2}, 1)$ and A and C are vertices of three edges (cases *b*, *c* or *d*). Now we may admit as adjacent face at AC a square (case *d*) or a triangle (cases *b* or *c*).

In the former hypothesis, let ACDE be that adjacent square. Then ABE and CBD are adjacent faces of ABC. Hence, as $BDC = BEA = \beta$, D and E are vertices of 3 edges. Thus the polyhedron is closed, and there is no room for triangle $(1, 1, 1)$.

In the latter hypothesis, let ACF be the adjacent triangle. Then we get a tetrahedron, and there is no room for a square.

Case **B.** Combination C_5, tC_5, C_{24}.

The bounding faces of the edge polyhedron are:

Triangle $(1, 1, 1)$ with the angles $(1, 1) = \alpha$,
" $(\sqrt{2}, \sqrt{2}, 1)$ " " " $(\sqrt{2}, \sqrt{2}) = \alpha$, $(\sqrt{2}, 1) = \beta$,
" $(\sqrt{2}, \sqrt{2}, \sqrt{2})$ " " " $(\sqrt{2}, \sqrt{2}) = \gamma$.

We can admit the following vertices:

a). $(\sqrt{2}, \sqrt{2}, \sqrt{2})$ . . . . . (α, α, α),
b). $(\sqrt{2}, \sqrt{2}, \sqrt{2})$ . . . . . (α, α, γ),
c). $(\sqrt{2}, \sqrt{2}, \sqrt{2})$ . . . . . (α, γ, γ),
d). $(\sqrt{2}, \sqrt{2}, 1)$ . . . . . . (β, β, α),
e). $(\sqrt{2}, \sqrt{2}, 1)$ . . . . . . (β, β, γ),
f). $(\sqrt{2}, 1, 1)$ . . . . (α, β, β),
g). $(\sqrt{2}, \sqrt{2}, \sqrt{2}, \sqrt{2})$ . . . $(\alpha, \alpha, \alpha, \alpha)$,
h). $(\sqrt{2}, \sqrt{2}, \sqrt{2}, \sqrt{2})$ . . . $(\alpha, \alpha, \alpha, \gamma)$,
i). $(1, 1, 1, 1)$ . . . . $(\alpha, \alpha, \alpha, \alpha)$.

In order to demonstrate that this case must be rejected, let ABC be a bounding triangle, $AB = BC = \sqrt{2}$, $AC = 1$. Again A and C are vertices of 3 edges (cases *d*, *e* or *f*). As all the bounding faces are triangles the polyhedron is a tetrahedron ABCD. But now we have to consider the following cases:

$$AD = CD = 1,$$
$$AD = CD = \sqrt{2}.$$

In the former case BD must be $= \sqrt{2}$, so there is no triangle $(\sqrt{2}, \sqrt{2}, \sqrt{2})$.

In the latter case BD may be $= \sqrt{2}$ or $= 1$. But anyhow, there is no triangle $(1, 1, 1)$.

Case **C.** Combination C_{16}, tC_5, C_{24}.

The faces bounding the edge polyhedron are:

squares $(1, 1, 1, 1)$ with the angles $(1, 1) = \gamma$,
triangles $(\sqrt{2}, \sqrt{2}, 1)$ " " " $(\sqrt{2}, \sqrt{2}) = \alpha$, $(\sqrt{2}, 1) = \beta$,
" $(\sqrt{2}, \sqrt{2}, \sqrt{2})$ " " " $(\sqrt{2}, \sqrt{2}) = \gamma$.

We can admit the following vertices:

a). $(\sqrt{2}, \sqrt{2}, \sqrt{2})$ . . . . . . (α, α, α),
b). $(\sqrt{2}, \sqrt{2}, \sqrt{2})$ . . . . . . (α, α, γ),
c). $(\sqrt{2}, \sqrt{2}, \sqrt{2})$ . . . . . . (α, γ, γ),
d). $(\sqrt{2}, \sqrt{2}, 1)$ . . . . . . (β, β, α),
e). $(\sqrt{2}, \sqrt{2}, 1)$ . . . . . . (β, β, γ),
f). $(1, 1, \sqrt{2})$ . . . . (β, β, γ),
g). $(\sqrt{2}, \sqrt{2}, \sqrt{2}, \sqrt{2})$ . . . . $(\alpha, \alpha, \alpha, \alpha)$,
h). $(\sqrt{2}, \sqrt{2}, \sqrt{2}, \sqrt{2})$ . . . $(\alpha, \alpha, \alpha, \gamma)$.

We will demonstrate that this case cannot be realized. Let us consider a bounding square. Its vertices can belong to case *f* only, and consequently its adjacent faces are triangles $(\sqrt{2}, \sqrt{2}, 1)$. Hence the polyhedron is a 4-angular pyramid, where triangle $(\sqrt{2}, \sqrt{2}, \sqrt{2})$ is wholly excluded.

Four kinds of bounding cells.

§ 33. The only possible combination of four bounding cells is

$$C_5, C_{16}, C_{24}, tC_5.$$

The faces of the edge polyhedron are:

triangles $(1, 1, 1)$ with the angles $(1, 1) = \alpha$,
squares $(1, 1, 1, 1)$ „ „ „ $(1, 1) = \gamma$,
triangles $(\sqrt{2}, \sqrt{2}, \sqrt{2})$ „ „ „ $(\sqrt{2}, \sqrt{2}) = \gamma$,
„ $(\sqrt{2}, \sqrt{2}, 1)$ „ „ „ $(\sqrt{2}, \sqrt{2}) = \alpha$ and $(\sqrt{2}, 1) = \beta$.

We can admit the following vertices:

a). $(\sqrt{2}, \sqrt{2}, \sqrt{2})$ . . . . (α, α, α),
b). $(\sqrt{2}, \sqrt{2}, \sqrt{2})$ . . . . (α, α, γ),
c). $(\sqrt{2}, \sqrt{2}, \sqrt{2})$ . . . . (α, γ, γ),
d). $(\sqrt{2}, \sqrt{2}, 1)$ . . . . (β, β, α),
e). $(\sqrt{2}, \sqrt{2}, 1)$. . . . . (β, β, γ),
f). $(1, 1, \sqrt{2})$ . . . . (β, β, α),
g). $(1, 1, \sqrt{2})$ . . . . (β, β, γ),
h). $(1, 1, 1)$ . . . . (α, α, α),
i). $(1, 1, 1)$ . . . . (α, α, γ),

j). $(1, 1, 1)$ . . . . (α, γ, γ),
k). $(\sqrt{2}, \sqrt{2}, \sqrt{2}, \sqrt{2})$ . . . $(\alpha, \alpha, \alpha, \alpha)$,
l). $(\sqrt{2}, \sqrt{2}, \sqrt{2}, \sqrt{2})$ . . . $(\alpha, \alpha, \alpha, \gamma)$,
m). $(1, 1, 1, 1)$ . . . . $(\alpha, \alpha, \alpha, \alpha)$,
n). $(1, 1, 1, 1)$ . . . . $(\alpha, \alpha, \alpha, \gamma)$.

This case must also be rejected. Indeed, let ABC be a bounding triangle, $AB = BC = \sqrt{2}$, $AC = 1$. Then A and C may represent one of the cases *d*, *e*, *f* and *g*, and the adjacent faces at AB and BC are triangles $(\sqrt{2}, \sqrt{2}, 1)$ or $(\sqrt{2}, \sqrt{2}, \sqrt{2})$. The adjacent face at AC may be a square, or one of the triangles $(\sqrt{2}, \sqrt{2}, 1)$ and $(1, 1, 1)$. In the former hypothesis, let ACDE be that adjacent square; then $BE = BD = \sqrt{2}$. The vertices E and D represent case *g* and we can pass no other edge through them. The polyhedron is closed, and both $(1, 1, 1)$ and $(\sqrt{2}, \sqrt{2}, \sqrt{2})$ are wanting. In the latter hypothesis, the polyhedron is a tetrahedron and the square is wholly excluded.

(20, 90, 120, 60, 12). § 34. We will now show that the cases, which have not been rejected, in the preceding arts., really correspond to existing polytopes.

We can construct the polytope

$$(20, 90, 120, 60, 12)$$

of art. 30 by joining the centres of the faces of a regular simplex $E_1E_2E_3E_4E_5E_6$.

The centre of $E_1E_2E_3$ will be represented by

$$E_{123}.$$

Thus $r_0 = (6)_3 = 20$.

Through the corresponding face $E_1E_2E_3$ pass the following T:

$$E_1E_2E_3E_4, \quad E_1E_2E_3E_5, \quad E_1E_2E_3E_6,$$

and in any of these T we can draw 3 edges through E_{123} viz. in $E_1E_2E_3E_4$ from E_{123} to E_{124}, E_{134} and E_{234}, etc. The edge $E_{123}E_{124}$ will be represented by

$$K_{\overset{+}{1}\overset{+}{2}34}.$$

Hence $r_1 = (6)_4 \cdot (4)_2 = 90$, and 9 edges pass through a vertex.

We will now immediately determine the bounding cells. Any $(C_5)_{\overset{-}{6}}$ is transformed into a tC_5 which will be indicated by

$$(tC_5)_{\overset{-}{6}}.$$

Any $T(E_1E_2E_3E_4)$ bounding $(C_5)_{\overset{-}{6}}$ is transformed into a similar T, whose vertices are

$$E_{123}, \quad E_{124}, \quad E_{134}, \quad E_{234},$$

and which we will represent by

$$T_{\overset{-}{5}\overset{-}{6}}.$$

The O which truncates $(C_5)_{\overset{-}{6}}$ at E_5 has for vertices

$$E_{125},$$
$$E_{134}, \quad E_{145}, \quad E_{245}, \quad E_{235},$$
$$E_{345},$$

and will be represented by

$$O_{\overset{+}{5}\overset{-}{6}}.$$

Thus the truncated cell $(tC_5)_{\overset{-}{6}}$ is bounded by

$$O_{\overset{+}{1}\overset{-}{6}}, \quad O_{\overset{+}{2}\overset{-}{6}}, \quad O_{\overset{+}{3}\overset{-}{6}}, \quad O_{\overset{+}{4}\overset{-}{6}}, \quad O_{\overset{+}{5}\overset{-}{6}},$$
$$T_{\overset{-}{1}\overset{-}{6}}, \quad T_{\overset{-}{2}\overset{-}{6}}, \quad T_{\overset{-}{3}\overset{-}{6}}, \quad T_{\overset{-}{4}\overset{-}{6}}, \quad T_{\overset{-}{5}\overset{-}{6}},$$

where any O has a face in common with any other O and with any T except with the one having the same subscripts.

In that tC_5 the homogeneous face between $O_{\overset{+}{1}\overset{-}{6}}$ and $O_{\overset{+}{2}\overset{-}{6}}$ has for vertices and edges:

$$E_{123}, \quad E_{124}, \quad E_{125},$$
$$K_{\overset{+}{1}\overset{+}{2}45}, \quad K_{\overset{+}{1}\overset{+}{2}35}, \quad K_{\overset{+}{1}\overset{+}{2}34},$$

and is represented by

$$F_{\overset{+}{1}\overset{+}{2}\overset{-}{6}}.$$

The number of these faces is $(6)_3 \cdot (3)_2 = 60$.

The heterogeneous face, in the same cell, between $O_{\overset{+}{1}\overset{-}{6}}$ and $T_{\overset{-}{2}\overset{-}{6}}$, the vertices and edges of which are

$$E_{145},\quad E_{135},\quad E_{134},$$
$$K_{\overset{+}{1}\overset{+}{3}45},\quad K_{\overset{+}{1}\overset{+}{3}45},\quad K_{\overset{+}{1}34\overset{+}{5}},$$

is represented by

$$F_{\overset{+}{1}\overset{-}{2}\overset{-}{6}}.$$

The number of these faces is 60.

The truncating cell at the vertex E_1 will be represented by

$$(tC_5)_{\overset{+}{1}}.$$

We can obtain its bounding O by determining the O which truncate $(C_5)_{\overset{-}{2}}$, $(C_5)_{\overset{-}{3}}$, $(C_5)_{\overset{-}{4}}$, $(C_5)_{\overset{-}{5}}$ and $(C_5)_{\overset{-}{6}}$ at E_1. So they are

$$O_{\overset{+}{1}\overset{-}{2}},\quad O_{\overset{+}{1}\overset{-}{3}},\quad O_{\overset{+}{1}\overset{-}{4}},\quad O_{\overset{+}{1}\overset{-}{5}},\quad O_{\overset{+}{1}\overset{-}{6}}.$$

The vertices of a T bounding that cell are the centres of the 4 faces of the simplex, that pass through an edge through E_1. Taking for instance the edge E_1E_6 we find

$$E_{126},\quad E_{136},\quad E_{146},\quad E_{156}$$

and the T with these vertices will be represented by

$$T_{\overset{+}{1}\overset{+}{6}}.$$

Thus the bounding T of $(tC_5)_{\overset{+}{1}}$ are

$$T_{\overset{+}{1}\overset{+}{2}},\quad T_{\overset{+}{1}\overset{+}{3}},\quad T_{\overset{+}{1}\overset{+}{4}},\quad T_{\overset{+}{1}\overset{+}{5}},\quad T_{\overset{+}{1}\overset{+}{6}}.$$

The homogeneous face in that cell between $O_{\overset{+}{1}\overset{-}{5}}$ and $O_{\overset{+}{1}\overset{-}{6}}$ is $F_{\overset{+}{1}\overset{-}{5}\overset{-}{6}}$; the heterogeneous face between $O_{\overset{+}{1}\overset{-}{6}}$ and $T_{\overset{+}{1}\overset{+}{5}}$ is $F_{\overset{+}{1}\overset{+}{5}\overset{-}{6}}$.

Thus $r_2 = 60 + 60 = 120$.

The number of $O_{\overset{+}{1}\overset{-}{6}}$ being 30, that of both $T_{\overset{+}{1}\overset{+}{6}}$ and $T_{\overset{-}{1}\overset{-}{6}}$ being 15, we have $r_3 = 60$.

We may call the O *quasi-heterogeneous* bodies.

It appears that the faces, though differently notated, are equal. Indeed

through F^{++-}_{156} pass O^{+-}_{15}, O^{+-}_{16}, T^{++}_{15} and $(tC_5)^{+}_{1}$, $(tC_5)^{+}_{5}$, $(tC_5)^{-}_{6}$,

" F^{--+}_{156} " O^{-+}_{15}, O^{-+}_{16}, T^{--}_{15} " $(tC_5)^{-}_{1}$, $(tC_5)^{-}_{5}$, $(tC_5)^{+}_{6}$.

Any face is heterogeneous in 2 tC_5, homogeneous in 1 tC_5.

The edges are equal. Through K^{++}_{1234} pass

F^{++-}_{126}, F^{++-}_{125}, F^{+--}_{156}, F^{+--}_{256},

T^{++}_{12},

O^{+-}_{26}, O^{+-}_{25}, O^{+-}_{15}, O^{+-}_{16},

T^{--}_{56},

$(tC_5)^{-}_{5}$, $(tC_5)^{-}_{6}$, $(tC_5)^{+}_{2}$, $(tC_5)^{+}_{1}$.

Hence the edge polyhedron is bounded by 4 triangles $(\sqrt{2}, \sqrt{2}, 1)$. Two opposite edges are $= 1$, the other edges $= \sqrt{2}$. Its degree of regularity is $\frac{1}{3}$.

We stated before that 9 edges pass through any vertex of the polytope. Hence the vertex polytope admits 9 vertices. Through any of these vertices pass 4 edges, 6 faces (2 triangles and 4 squares) and 4 P_3. Hence we get the prismotope (9, 18, 15, 6) whose degree of regularity is $\frac{1}{2}$.

As the faces of the polytope are equal, *its degree of regularity is* $\frac{3}{5}$.

(16, 80, 160, 120, 26). § 35. We can derive the polytope

(16, 80, 160, 120, 26)

(art. 31, A, *b*) from the measure polytope.

Let a vertex of the measure polytope be represented by

E[+ + + + +],

then we will represent a vertex of the derived polytope by

E}+ + + + +{.

The } { indicate that the other vertices can be obtained by applying all the permutations on the given symbol and by changing an *even* number of signs. (The permutations are only of consequence in a case where a set of different coordinates are included). Hence $r_0 = \frac{1}{2} \cdot 2^5 = 16$. The polytope will be called *half measure polytope.*

It is obvious that we can derive an other from the same measure polytope, the vertices of which are represented by

E}+ + + + −{.

Thus a C bounding the measure polytope is transformed into T, a bounding C_8 into C_{16}.

It is obvious that the edges are diagonals of the squares which bound the measure polytope, only one diagonal in any square. Now, through

E[+ + + + +]

pass 10 squares viz.

F[0 0 + + +]

and those, which result from that symbol by arranging the 0 and the + differently. Hence through a vertex pass 10 edges.

The edge which is a diagonal of F[0 0 + + +] and which joins E}+ + + + +{ to E}− − + + +{ will be represented by

K}(0 0 + + +){ [1]).

Hence $r_1 = 80$.

---

1) Here we keep the } {, though it is of no consequence. Indeed we are allowed to change an odd number of signs and to imagine ourselves that we changed a zero besides.

The face, which truncates $C[++000]$ at $E\}+++--\{$, and which we will represent by

$$F\Big\}\begin{smallmatrix}+\,+\\+\,+\end{smallmatrix}++-\Big\{,$$

has for vertices and edges

$$E\}++-+-\{,\quad E\}+++--\{,\quad E\}+++++\{,$$
$$K\}+++00\{,\quad K\}++0+0\{,\quad K\}++00-\{.$$

The number of the faces is $16\,.\,(5)_2 = 160$.

We will now consider the truncated cells. $C_8[+0000]$ is transformed into a C_{16}, which we will represent by

$$C_{16}\}+0000\{.$$

That C_8 is truncated at $\}++++-\{$ by a T whose vertices are

$$E\}+-++-\{,\quad E\}++-+-\{,\quad E\}+++--\{,$$
$$E\}+++++\{,$$

and which we will represent by

$$T\Big\}\begin{smallmatrix}+\\+\end{smallmatrix}+++-\Big\{.$$

The $C[++000]$ bounding the same C_8 is transformed into a T, which we will represent by

$$T\}++000\{;$$

its vertices and faces are

$$E\}+++++\{,\quad E\}+++--\{,\quad E\}++-+-\{,$$
$$E\}++--+\{,$$

$$F\Big\}\begin{smallmatrix}+\,+\\+\,+\end{smallmatrix}---\Big\{,\quad F\Big\}\begin{smallmatrix}+\,+\\+\,+\end{smallmatrix}-++\Big\{,\quad F\Big\}\begin{smallmatrix}+\,+\\+\,+\end{smallmatrix}++-\Big\{,$$

$$F\Big\}\begin{smallmatrix}+\,+\\+\,+\end{smallmatrix}++-\Big\{.$$

The number of the truncating T is 80, that of the truncated T is 40.

The cell which truncates the measure polytope at $E\}++++-\{$ will be represented by

$$C_5\}++++-\{,$$

and has the following vertices:

$E\{-+++-\}$, $E\{+-++-\}$, $E\{++-+-\}$,
$E\{+++--\}$, $E\{+++++\}$.

The bounding T are:

$$T\left\{\substack{+\\+}+++-\right\},\quad T\left\{+\substack{+\\+}++-\right\},\quad T\left\{++\substack{+\\+}+-\right\},$$

$$T\left\{+++\substack{+\\+}-\right\},\quad T\left\{++++\substack{-\\-}\right\}.$$

The truncating T are heterogeneous, the truncated T homogeneous. Indeed through

$T\{++000\}$ pass $C_{16}\{+0000\}$ and $C_{16}\{0+000\}$,
$T\left\{\substack{+\\+}+++-\right\}$ „ $C_{16}\{+0000\}$ „ $C_5\{++++-\}$.

The faces are equal. Through

$$F\left\{\substack{++\\++}++-\right\}$$

pass

$T\left\{\substack{+\\+}+++-\right\}$, $T\left\{+\substack{+\\+}++-\right\}$, $T\{++000\}$,
$C_{16}\{0+000\}$, $C_{16}\{+0000\}$, $C_6\{++++-\}$.

Hence the faces are isosceles.

The edges are equal. Through $K\{00+++\}$ pass

$$F\left\{++\substack{++\\++}+\right\},\quad F\left\{++\substack{+\\+}+\substack{+\\+}\right\},\quad F\left\{+++\substack{++\\++}\right\},$$

$$F\left\{--\substack{++\\++}+\right\},\quad F\left\{--\substack{+\\+}+\substack{+\\+}\right\},\quad F\left\{--+\substack{++\\++}\right\},$$

$$T\left\{++++\substack{+\\+}\right\},\quad T\left\{+++\substack{+\\+}+\right\},\quad T\left\{++\substack{+\\+}++\right\},$$

$$T\{00++0\},\quad T\{00+0+\},\quad T\{000++\},$$

$$T\left\{--++\substack{+\\+}\right\},\quad T\left\{--+\substack{+\\+}+\right\},\quad T\left\{--\substack{+\\+}++\right\},$$

$$C_5\{+++++\},$$

$$C_{16}\{0000+\},\quad C_{16}\{000+0\},\quad C_{16}\{00+00\},$$

$$C_5\{+++++\}.$$

Hence the edge polyhedron is P_3. As 10 edges pass through any vertex of the polytope, the vertex polytope is tC_5.

The polytope has equal vertices, edges and faces. It is

wholly bounded by T. There are two kinds of the latter. Hence *its degree of regularity is* $\frac{7}{10}$.

(15, 60, 80, 45, 12). § 36. We can obtain the polytope of art. 31, B by joining the midpoints of the edges of a regular simplex.

Let E_1, E_2, E_3, E_4, E_5 and E_6 represent the vertices of that simplex, then we will indicate by

$$E_{12}$$

the midpoint of E_1E_2. Hence $r_0 = 15$.

Through E_1E_2 pass the faces

$$E_1E_2E_3,\quad E_1E_2E_4,\quad E_1E_2E_5,\quad E_1E_2E_6,$$

and in any of these faces we can draw 2 edges through E_{12}. Hence 8 edges pass through any vertex of the polytope.

The edge $E_{12}E_{13}$ will be represented by

$$E_{1|23}$$

Hence $r_1 = 3 \,.\, (6)_3 = 60$.

Any $(C_5)_{\overline{6}}$ which bounds the simplex is transformed into a tC_5, which we will represent by

$$(tC_5)_{\overline{6}}.$$

In that cell the O, into which $T(E_2E_3E_4E_5)$ is transformed, has the following vertices

$$E_{23},$$
$$E_{24},\quad E_{34},\quad E_{35},\quad E_{25},$$
$$E_{45},$$

and will be denoted by

$$O_{\overline{1}\,\overline{6}}.$$

The T which truncates $(C_5)_{\overline{6}}$ at E_1 is bounded by

$$E_{12},\quad E_{13},\quad E_{14},\quad E_{15},$$

and will be represented by

$$T_{1|\overline{6}}.$$

So the following bodies bound $(tC_5)_{\bar{6}}$:

$$O_{\bar{1}\bar{6}},\quad O_{\bar{2}\bar{6}},\quad O_{\bar{3}\bar{6}},\quad O_{\bar{4}\bar{6}},\quad O_{\bar{5}\bar{6}},$$

$$T_{\overset{+}{1}\bar{6}},\quad T_{\overset{+}{2}\bar{6}},\quad T_{\overset{+}{3}\bar{6}},\quad T_{\overset{+}{4}\bar{6}},\quad T_{\overset{+}{5}\bar{6}}.$$

The numbers of these O and T are 15 and 30 respectively.

The homogeneous face, in that tC_5, between $O_{\bar{1}\bar{6}}$ and $O_{\bar{2}\bar{6}}$, has for vertices and edges

$$E_{34},\quad E_{35},\quad E_{45},\qquad \text{and}\qquad K_{34\overset{+}{5}},\quad K_{3\overset{+}{4}5},\quad K_{\overset{+}{3}45},$$

and is represented by

$$F_{345}.$$

The number of these faces is 20.

The heterogeneous face, in the same tC_5, between $O_{\bar{1}\bar{6}}$ and $T_{\overset{+}{2}\bar{6}}$, has for vertices and edges

$$E_{23},\quad E_{24},\quad E_{25},\qquad \text{and}\qquad K_{\overset{+}{2}45},\quad K_{\overset{+}{2}35},\quad K_{\overset{+}{2}34},$$

and is represented by

$$F_{\overset{+}{2}345}.$$

The number of these faces is $(6)_4 \cdot 4 = 60$.

We will now consider the truncating cells. At E_1 we get a C_5 whose vertices are

$$E_{12},\quad E_{13},\quad E_{15},\quad E_{14},\quad E_{16},$$

and which we represent by

$$(C_5)_{\overset{+}{1}}.$$

Its bounding T belong to those mentioned above, viz.

$$T_{\overset{+}{1}\bar{2}},\quad T_{\overset{+}{1}\bar{3}},\quad T_{\overset{+}{1}\bar{4}},\quad T_{\overset{+}{1}\bar{5}},\quad T_{\overset{+}{1}\bar{6}}$$

and its faces belong to the heterogeneous faces mentioned above.

There are two kinds of bounding polyhedra viz. T and O. The former are heterogeneous (between tC_5 and C_5); the latter are homogeneous (between two tC_5). Indeed through $O_{\bar{1}\bar{6}}$ pass $(tC_5)_{\bar{1}}$ and $(tC_5)_{\bar{6}}$,

" $T_{\overset{+}{1}\bar{2}}$ " $(tC_5)_{\bar{2}}$ " $(C_5)_{\overset{+}{1}}$.

The faces are different. Those of 4 subscripts are isosceles. Through $F_{\overset{+}{2}345}$ pass

$T_{\bar{1}\overset{+}{2}}$, $T_{\overset{+}{2}\bar{6}}$, $O_{\bar{1}\bar{6}}$, and $(tC_5)_{\bar{6}}$, $(tC_5)_{\bar{1}}$, $(C_5)_{\overset{+}{2}}$.

Those of the other kind are equilateral. Through F_{345} pass

$O_{\bar{1}\bar{6}}$, $O_{\bar{2}\bar{6}}$, $O_{\bar{1}\bar{2}}$, and $(tC_5)_{\bar{2}}$, $(tC_5)_{\bar{1}}$, $(tC_5)_{\bar{6}}$.

With regard to the faces the polytope shows $\frac{1}{2}$ characteristic of regularity.

The edges are equal. Through $K_{\overset{+}{1}23}$ pass

F_{123},

$F_{\overset{+}{1}234}$, $F_{\overset{+}{1}235}$, $F_{\overset{+}{1}236}$,

$O_{\bar{5}\bar{6}}$, $O_{\bar{4}\bar{6}}$, $O_{\bar{4}\bar{5}}$,

$T_{\overset{+}{1}\bar{4}}$, $T_{\overset{+}{1}\bar{5}}$, $T_{\overset{+}{1}\bar{6}}$,

$(tC_5)_{\bar{4}}$, $(tC_5)_{\bar{5}}$, $(tC_5)_{\bar{6}}$,

$(C_5)_{\overset{+}{1}}$.

Hence the edge polyhedron is a tetrahedron bounded by one equilateral triangle (1, 1, 1) and 3 triangles ($\sqrt{2}$, $\sqrt{2}$, 1), and consequently by three edges 1 (the sides of the equilateral triangle) and 3 edges $\sqrt{2}$ meeting at one vertex. Thus it shows no characteristic of regularity.

Through any vertex of the polytope pass 8 edges. Hence the vertices are equal. We infer from the structure of the edge polyhedron that, in the vertex polytope, any vertex belongs to 1T and 3 P_3. The number of vertices being 8, we get a regular prism P_T whose bases are T, at a distance unity from each other. Its degree of regularity is $\frac{3}{8}$.

The degree of regularity of the polytope is $\frac{1}{2}$.

(4C, 240, 400, 240, 42). § 37. The bounding elements of the cross polytope are

$$E[+\ 0\ \ 0\ \ 0\ \ 0\,],$$
$$K[+\ +\ 0\ \ 0\ \ 0\,],$$
$$F[+\ +\ +\ 0\ \ 0\,],$$
$$T[+\ +\ +\ +\ 0\,],$$
$$C_5[+\ +\ +\ +\ +].$$

Now we can obtain the polytope of art. 31, C by joining the midpoints of the edges of the cross polytope. Its vertices are represented by

$$E[+\ +0\,0\,0].$$

Hence $r_0 = (5)_2 \,.\, 4 = 40$.

In order to determine the edges through a vertex, we remark that through the corresponding edge K[+ +000] of the cross polytope pass the following faces

$$F[+\ +\ +0\,0],\qquad F[+\ +0+0],\qquad F[+\ +0\,0\,+],$$
$$F[+\ +\ -0\,0],\qquad F[+\ +0-0],\qquad F[+\ +0\,0\,-],$$

and that in any of these faces we can draw 2 edges through E[+ +000]. One of these edges joins that vertex to E[+0+00] and is represented by

$$K\left[\begin{matrix}+\\+\end{matrix}\ +\ +\ 0\,0\right].$$

Hence $r_1 = (5)_3 \,.\, 8 \,.\, 3 = 240$.

C_5[+ + + + +] is transformed into a tC_5, which we represent by

$$tC_5[+\ +\ +\ +\ +].$$

The O, into which T[+ + + + 0] is transformed, has for vertices

$$E[+\ +0\,0\,0],$$
$$E[+\,0+0\,0],\ \ E[0+\,+0\,0],\ \ E[0+0+0],\ \ E[+\,0\,0+0],$$
$$E[0\,0+\,+0],$$

and will be represented by

$$O[+\ +\ +\ +0].$$

The number of O is 80.

The T which truncates C_5[+ + + + +] at E[+0000] has the following vertices:

E[+ + 0 0 0], E[+ 0 + 0 0], E[+ 0 0 + 0], E[+ 0 0 0 +],
and will be represented by

$$T\left[\substack{+\\+} + + + +\right].$$

The number of T is 160.

Thus tC_5[+ + + + +] is bounded by the following bodies:

O[0 + + + +], O[+ 0 + + +], O[+ + 0 + +],
O[+ + + 0 +], O[+ + + + 0],

$$T\left[\substack{+\\+} + + + +\right],\quad T\left[+ \substack{+\\+} + + +\right],\quad T\left[+ + \substack{+\\+} + +\right],$$

$$T\left[+ + + \substack{+\\+} +\right],\quad T\left[+ + + + \substack{+\\+}\right].$$

The homogeneous face, in that tC_5, between O[+ + + + 0] and O[+ + + 0 +], admits the vertices and edges

E[+ + 0 0 0], E[+ 0 + 0 0], E[0 + + 0 0],

$$K\left[+ + \substack{+\\+} 0\,0\right],\quad K\left[+ \substack{+\\+} + 0\,0\right],\quad K\left[\substack{+\\+} + + 0\,0\right],$$

and will be represented by

F[+ + + 0 0].

The number of those faces is 80.

The heterogeneous face, in the same tC_5, between O[+ + + + 0] and $T\left[+ + + \substack{+\\+} +\right]$, has the vertices and edges

E[+ 0 0 + 0], E[0 + 0 + 0], E[0 0 + + 0],

$$K\left[0 + + \substack{+\\+} 0\right],\quad K\left[+ 0 + \substack{+\\+} 0\right],\quad K\left[+ + 0 \substack{+\\+} 0\right],$$

and is represented by

$$F\left[+ + + \substack{+\\+} 0\right].$$

Their number is 320.

The truncating cells are C_{16}. That which truncates the cross polytcpe at E[+ 0 0 0 0] will be represented by

C_{16}[+ 0 0 0 0]

and has the following vertices:

E[+ + 0 0 0], E[+ 0 + 0 0], E[+ 0 0 + 0], E[+ 0 0 0 +],
E[+ — 0 0 0], E[+ 0 — 0 0], E[+ 0 0 — 0], E[+ 0 0 0 —].

It appears that the truncating cells have the T in common with the truncated ones, and that an O belongs to two tC_5.

Through $O[++++0]$ pass $tC_5[+++++]$ and $tC_5[++++-]$.

Through $T\left[{}^{+}_{+}++++\right]$ pass $tC_5[+++++]$ and $C_{16}[+0000]$.

The faces are unequal.

Through $F[+++00]$ pass

$$O[++++0],\quad O[+++0+],\quad O[+++-0],\quad O[+++0-],$$

$$tC_5[+++++],\quad tC_5[+++-+],\quad tC_5[+++--],\quad tC_5[++++-].$$

So these faces are regular (i. e. the intersection with a three-dimensional space perpendicular to such a face is a regular tetrahedral angle).

Through $F\left[{}^{+}_{+}+++0\right]$ pass

$$O[++++0],\quad T\left[{}^{+}_{+}++++\right],\quad T\left[{}^{+}_{+}+++-\right],$$

$$C_{16}[+0000],\quad tC_5[++++-],\quad tC_5[+++++].$$

Thus these faces are isosceles.

The edges are equal. Through $K\left[{}^{+}_{+}++00\right]$ pass

$$F[+++00],$$

$$F\left[{}^{+}_{+}+++0\right],\quad F\left[{}^{+}_{+}++0+\right],\quad F\left[{}^{+}_{+}++-0\right],\quad F\left[{}^{+}_{+}++0-\right],$$

$$O[++++0],\quad O[+++0+],\quad O[+++-0],\quad O[+++0-],$$

$$T\left[{}^{+}_{+}++++\right],\quad T\left[{}^{+}_{+}++-+\right],\quad T\left[{}^{+}_{+}++--\right],\quad T\left[{}^{+}_{+}+++-\right],$$

$$tC_5[+++++],\quad tC_5[+++-+],\quad tC_5[+++--],$$
$$tC_5[++++-],$$
$$C_{16}[+\,0\,0\,0\,0].$$

Hence the edge polyhedron is bounded by 1 square (1, 1, 1, 1) and 4 triangles ($\sqrt{2}$, $\sqrt{2}$, 1) meeting at one vertex, which corresponds to a regular face. So it is a regular 4-angular pyramid, whose lateral edges are $=\sqrt{2}$ and whose base edges are $= 1$. It has no characteristic of regularity.

The vertex polytope has 12 vertices, and from the structure of the edge polyhedron we infer that through any of its vertices pass 4 P_3 and 1O. It is a regular prism P_O whose bases are O, at a distance 1 from each other. It shows $1\frac{1}{2}$ characteristics of regularity.

The degree of regularity of the polytope is $\frac{1}{2}$.

We obtain the same polytope by joining the centres of the C which bound the measure polytope. Then the tC_5 are the truncating, the C_{16} the truncated cells.

(80, 480, 640. § 38. The centres of the faces of the cross polytope are
280, 42). the vertices of the polytope of art. 31, D. We will represent its vertices by

$$E[+++\,0\,0].$$

Hence $r_0 = (5)_3 \,.\, 8 = 80$.

Through the corresponding $F[+++\,0\,0]$ of the cross polytope pass the following spaces:

$$T[++++\,0],\quad T[+++\,0\,+],$$
$$T[+++-0],\quad T[+++\,0\,-],$$

and in any of these T we can draw 3 edges through $E[+++\,0\,0]$. The edge through that vertex and through $E[++\,0+0]$ is represented by

$$K\left[\begin{matrix}+\,+\\+\,+\end{matrix}\;+\,+\,0\right].$$

Hence $r_1 = (5)_1 \,.\, 16 \,.\, (4)_2 = 480$.

The truncated cells are tC_5. That, into which $C_5[+ + + + +]$ is transformed, will be represented by

$$tC_5[+ + + + +].$$

The T bounding that cel and having the vertices $E[0 + + + 0]$, $E[+ 0 + + 0]$, $E[+ + 0 + 0]$, $E[+ + + 0 0]$ will be represented by

$$T[+ + + + 0].$$

The number of these T is 80.

The O bounding that tC_5 and which truncates $C_5[+ + + + +]$ at $E[+ 0 0 0 0]$ has the following vertices:

$$E[+ + + 0 0],$$

$$E[+ + 0 + 0],\ E[+ 0 + + 0],\ E[+ 0 + 0 +],\ E[+ + 0 0 +],$$

$$E[+ 0 0 + +],$$

and is represented by

$$O\left[\begin{array}{c}+\\ +\end{array} + + + +\right].$$

The number of these O is 160.

So $tC_5[+ + + + +]$ has the following bounding bodies:

$$O\left[\begin{array}{c}+\\ +\end{array} + + + +\right],\ O\left[+ \begin{array}{c}+\\ +\end{array} + + +\right],\ O\left[+ + \begin{array}{c}+\\ +\end{array} + +\right],$$

$$O\left[+ + + \begin{array}{c}+\\ +\end{array} +\right],\ O\left[+ + + + \begin{array}{c}+\\ +\end{array}\right],$$

$$T[0 + + + +],\ T[+ 0 + + +],\ T[+ + 0 + +],$$

$$T[+ + + 0 +],\ T[+ + + + 0].$$

The homogeneous face, in that tC_5, between $O\left[\begin{array}{c}+\\ +\end{array} + + + +\right]$ and $O\left[+ \begin{array}{c}+\\ +\end{array} + + +\right]$, has for vertices and edges

$$E[+ + + 0 0],\ E[+ + 0 + 0],\ E[+ + 0 0 +],$$

$$K\left[\begin{array}{cc}+ & +\\ + & +\end{array} 0 + +\right],\ K\left[\begin{array}{cc}+ & +\\ + & +\end{array} + 0 +\right],\ K\left[\begin{array}{cc}+ & +\\ + & +\end{array} + + 0\right],$$

and can be represented by

$$F\left[\begin{array}{cc}+ & +\\ + & +\end{array} + + +\right].$$

The number of these faces is $(5)_2 \,.\, 32 = 320$.

The heterogeneous face in the same tC_5, between $O\left[\begin{smallmatrix}+\\+\end{smallmatrix}\ + + + +\right]$ and $T[+0++ +]$, admits the vertices and edges

$$E[+0\,0\,++],\quad E[+0+0+],\quad E[+0++0],$$

$$K\left[\begin{smallmatrix}+\\+\end{smallmatrix}0\begin{smallmatrix}+\\+\end{smallmatrix}++\right],\quad K\left[\begin{smallmatrix}+\\+\end{smallmatrix}0+\begin{smallmatrix}+\\+\end{smallmatrix}+\right],\quad K\left[\begin{smallmatrix}+\\+\end{smallmatrix}0++\begin{smallmatrix}+\\+\end{smallmatrix}\right],$$

and will be represented by

$$F\left[\begin{smallmatrix}+\\+\end{smallmatrix}0+++\right].$$

The number of these faces is 320.

We will now endeavour to determine the truncating cells. The cell which truncates the cross polytope at

$$E[0\,0\,0\,0+]$$

is similar to the cell which can be constructed by joining the midpoints of the edges of the vertex polytope corresponding to $E[0\,0\,0\,0+]$, that vertex being the centre of similarity. So, as this vertex polytope is C_{16}, the truncating cells are C_{24}. And in order to determine the latter we will previously consider the C_{24} derived from the vertex polytope.

The vertices of the latter are:

$$E[+0\,0\,0\,0],\quad E[0+0\,0\,0],\quad E[0\,0+0\,0],$$
$$E[0\,0\,0+0],\quad E[0\,0\,0\,0+],$$
$$E[-0\,0\,0\,0],\quad E[0-0\,0\,0],\quad E[0\,0-0\,0],$$
$$E[0\,0\,0-0],\quad E[0\,0\,0\,0-].$$

Its bounding

$$T[++++0]$$

is transformed into a quasi-truncated O, whose vertices are

$$E[++0\,0\,0],$$
$$E[+0+0\,0],\quad E[+0\,0+0],\quad E[0+0+0],\quad E[0++0\,0],$$
$$E[0\,0++0],$$

and it is obvious that we obtain the corresponding O in the C_{24} which bounds the polytope by changing the fifth coordinates 0 into +.

Thus we represent that O by

$$O\left[+ + + + \substack{+ \\ +}\right].$$

The quasi-truncating O at E[+ 0 0 0 0] has the following vertices:

E[+ + 0 0 0],

E[+ 0 + 0 0], E[+ 0 0 + 0], E[+ 0 − 0 0], E[+ 0 0 − 0],

E[+ − 0 0 0].

Likewise we get the corresponding O in the C_{24} which bounds the polytope and represent it by

O[+ 0 0 0 +].

The bounding C_{24} is represented by

C_{24}[0 0 0 0 +].

In that C_{24} the quasi-heterogeneous face between $O\left[+ + + + \substack{+ \\ +}\right]$ and O[0 0 0 + +] has for vertices

E[+ 0 0 + +], E[0 + 0 + +], E[0 0 + + +].

So this is $F\left[+ + + \substack{+ + \\ + +}\right]$.

The homogeneous face, in the same C_{24}, between $O\left[+ + + + \substack{+ \\ +}\right]$ and $O\left[+ + + - \substack{+ \\ +}\right]$, has the following vertices:

E[+ + 0 0 +], E[+ 0 + 0 +], E[0 + + 0 +].

So this is $F\left[+ + + 0 \substack{+ \\ +}\right]$.

Comparing the polyhedra, we find:

$O\left[\substack{+ \\ +} + + + +\right]$ is heterogeneous and belongs to

tC_5[+ + + + +] and C_{24}[+ 0 0 0 0],

O[+ 0 0 0 +] is homogeneous and belongs to

C_{24}[+ 0 0 0 0] and C_{24}[0 0 0 0 +],

$T[++++0]$ is homogeneous and belongs to
$tC_5[+++++]$ and $C_5[++++-]$.

The faces are unequal.

Through $F\left[\genfrac{}{}{0pt}{}{++}{++}+++\right]$ pass

$$O\left[\genfrac{}{}{0pt}{}{+}{+}++++\right],\quad O\left[+\genfrac{}{}{0pt}{}{+}{+}+++\right],\quad O[++000],$$

$$C_{24}[0+000],\quad C_{24}[+0000],\quad tC_5[+++++].$$

So these faces are isosceles.

Through $F\left[\genfrac{}{}{0pt}{}{+}{+}0+++\right]$ pass

$$O\left[\genfrac{}{}{0pt}{}{+}{+}++++\right],\quad O\left[\genfrac{}{}{0pt}{}{+}{+}-+++\right],\quad T[+0+++],$$

$$tC_5[+-+++],\quad tC_5[+++++],\quad C_{24}[+0000].$$

So these faces are also isosceles.

The edges are equal. Through $K\left[\genfrac{}{}{0pt}{}{++}{++}++0\right]$ pass

$$F\left[\genfrac{}{}{0pt}{}{++}{++}+++\right],\quad F\left[\genfrac{}{}{0pt}{}{++}{++}++-\right],\quad F\left[\genfrac{}{}{0pt}{}{+}{+}+++0\right],$$

$$F\left[+\genfrac{}{}{0pt}{}{+}{+}++0\right],$$

$$O[++000],$$

$$O\left[\genfrac{}{}{0pt}{}{+}{+}++++\right],\quad O\left[+\genfrac{}{}{0pt}{}{+}{+}+++\right],\quad O\left[+\genfrac{}{}{0pt}{}{+}{+}++-\right],$$

$$O\left[\genfrac{}{}{0pt}{}{+}{+}+++-\right],$$

$$T[++++0],$$

$$tC_5[++++-],\quad tC_5[+++++],\quad C_{24}[0+000],$$
$$C_{24}[+0000].$$

Hence the edge polyhedron is a tetrahedron of which one edge is 1; the other edges $\sqrt{2}$. It shows no characteristic of regularity.

The vertex polytope has 12 vertices. Besides we infer from the structure of the vertex polytope that through a vertex pass 2 C and 2 P_3. Hence it is a prism whose bases P_3 are at a distance 1 from each other. Its degree of regularity is $\frac{3}{8}$.

The degree of regularity of the polytope is $\frac{1}{2}$.

We can obtain the same polytope by joining the centres of the squares forming the faces of a measure polytope.

CHAPTER V.

SIXDIMENSIONAL SEMIREGULAR POLYTOPES.

Preliminary. § 39. We will now determine the sixdimensional polytopes whose degree of regularity is at least $\frac{1}{2}$. As their faces must be equal, we cannot admit the measure polytope as bounding fivedimensional polytope. The following list, to which we will refer occasionally in the course of the investigation, contains the dihedral angles at the R_3 and the solid angles round the faces in S_5, Cr_5 and the fivedimensional semiregular polytopes. In the first column S_5^1 represents the polytope (15, 60, 80, 45, 12), the exponent 1 denoting that its vertices are the midpoints of the *edges* of S_5 etc. HM_5 represents the fivedimensional half measure polytope. In the second column the indices T and O, in the case of S_5^2, are to discern the couples of tC_6 that have a T and those that have an O in common. In the third column the faces are represented by the polytopes passing through them. In the cases of S_5^1, Cr_5^1 and Cr_5^2 the number of each kind of faces has been added between parentheses.

In this chapter we will use R_0, R_1, etc. for the bounding spaces of the sixdimensional polytopes, r_0, r_1, etc. for their vertex polytopes, E, K, F and R for their edge polytopes, and e, k and f for their face polyhedra. The latter do not indicate necessarily the degree of regularity of the face, as the edges of the edge polyhedra may be unequal.

	Dihedral angles	Solid angles round a face
S_5	78° 27′ 47″	55° 23′ 21″
Cr_5	126° 52′ 10″	147° 28′ 40″
S_5^1	(tC_5, tC_5) = 78° 27′ 47″ (C_5, tC_5) = 101° 32′ 13″	(20) (tC_5, tC_5, tC_5) = 55° 23′ 21″ (60) (tC_5, tC_5, C_5) = 101° 32′ 13″
S_5^2	$(tC_5, tC_5)_T$ = 78° 27′ 47″ $(tC_5, tC_5)_O$ = 101° 32′13″	101° 32′ 13′
Cr_5^2	(tC_5, tC_5) = 126° 52′ 10″ (C_{24}, tC_5) = 116° 33′ 55″ (C_{24}, C_{24}) = 90°	(320) (C_{24}, C_{24}, tC_5) = 143° 7′ 50″ (320) (C_{24}, tC_5, tC_5) = 180°
Cr_5^1	(tC_5, tC_5) = 126° 52′ 10″ (C_{16}, tC_5) = 116° 33′ 55″	(80) (tC_5, tC_5, tC_5, tC_5) = 147° 28′ 40″ (320) $tC_5, tC_5, C_{16})$ = 180°
HM_5	(C_{16}, C_{16}) = 90° (C_5, C_{16}) = 116° 33′ 55″	143° 7′ 50″

Exclusion of Cr_5^1.

§ 40. The following remark will simplify the discussion. Let a semiregular polytope be bounded by n S_5^1. The latter polytope has two kinds of solid angles viz. 20 equilateral and 60 isosceles ones. Let p be the number of equilateral, q that of isosceles solid angles at a face of the semiregular polytope. Then the number of the faces is $\frac{20n}{p}$ as well as $\frac{60n}{q}$, whence $q = 3p$. Hence we can, for the present, admit $p = 1$ and $q = 3$. The sum of solid angles is 55° 23′ 21″ + 3 × 101° 32′ 13″ = 360°. This reasoning holds too for a polytope bounded by S_5^1 in connection with others.

In the case of Cr_5^2 the numbers of the two kinds of faces are equal. Hence in order to bound a polytope by means of Cr_5^2 only, we want at least two of each kind of solid angles through a face. Combined with other polytopes we may admit one of each kind. In both cases the sum of solid angles does not exceed 720°.

In the case of Cr_5^1 the sum of solid angles would be at least $147^\circ 28' 40'' + 4 \times 180^\circ$. So this polytope must be rejected.

Reduced face polyhedron. § 41. It is convenient to replace, in this investigation the face polyhedron by an other, whose vertices are at a *unit* distance from a vertex of the edge polytope and situated in the edges through that vertex. We will call the thus defined polyhedron *reduced face polyhedron.* It is obvious that it is only different from the ordinary face polyhedron when the edges of the edge polytope are unequal. In the same way the face polygon of the fivedimensional polytopes can be replaced by the *reduced face polygon.* In the case of S_5^1, for instance, the face polygon corresponding to a face (tC_5, tC_5, tC_5) is a triangle, whose edges are equal to 1, while the edges through the corresponding vertex of the edge polyhedron are equal to $\sqrt{2}$. Now we will indicate the reduced face polygon by $(\sqrt{2}, \sqrt{2}, \sqrt{2})$. Thus the face polygon corresponding to a face (tC_5, tC_5, C_5) is a triangle whose edges are equal to $\sqrt{2}$, $\sqrt{2}$ and 1. Here the reduced face polygon must be represented by $(\sqrt{2}, 1, 1)$, according to the edges through the corresponding vertex of the edge polyhedron. The following list, where

$$\alpha = 78^\circ 27' 47'', \quad \beta = 126^\circ 52' 10'', \quad \gamma = 90^\circ, \quad \delta = 116^\circ 33' 55'',$$

contains the reduced face polygons and the corresponding dihedral angles.

S_5	$(1, 1, 1)$	(α, α, α)	
Cr_5	$(1, 1, 1, 1)$	$(\beta, \beta, \beta, \beta)$	
S_5^1	$(\sqrt{2}, \sqrt{2}, \sqrt{2})$	(α, α, α)	(20)
	$(\sqrt{2}, 1, 1)$	$(\alpha, 180° - \alpha, 180° - \alpha)$	(60)
S_5^2	$(1, \sqrt{2}, \sqrt{2})$	$(\alpha, 180° - \alpha, 180° - \alpha)$	
Cr_5^2	$(\sqrt{2}, \sqrt{2}, \sqrt{2})$	(γ, δ, δ)	(320)
	$(1, \sqrt{2}, \sqrt{2})$	(β, δ, δ)	(320)
HM_5	$(1, 1, 1)$	(γ, δ, δ).	

Exclusion of S_5^1, S_5^2 and Cr_5^2.

§ 42. Let a semiregular polytope be bounded by S_5^1. We can admit, in the reduced face polygon, one triangle $(\sqrt{2}, \sqrt{2}, \sqrt{2})$ and three triangles $(\sqrt{2}, 1, 1)$. We infer from the list that the adjacent faces of the former triangle can be

$(\sqrt{2}, \sqrt{2}, 1)$ belonging to S_5^2,
$(\sqrt{2}, \sqrt{2}, \sqrt{2})$ „ „ Cr_5^2,
$(\sqrt{2}, \sqrt{2}, 1)$ „ „ Cr_5^2.

We can admit only one of either of the two latter triangles (art. 40). So we can expect only one angle γ. Consequently, at least two of the vertices $\sqrt{2}$ are triangular. Hence the reduced face polyhedron is a tetrahedron. As it is impossible to build up a tetrahedron with one triangle $(\sqrt{2}, \sqrt{2}, \sqrt{2})$ and three triangles $(\sqrt{2}, 1, 1)$, S_5^1 must be rejected.

It is impossible to bound a polytope by means of Cr_5^2 only. Indeed this would require a tetrahedron bounded by two $(\sqrt{2}, \sqrt{2}, \sqrt{2})$ and two $(1, \sqrt{2}, \sqrt{2})$.

Let us try to combine Cr_5^2 with an other polytope and, for that purpose, consider $(\sqrt{2}, \sqrt{2}, \sqrt{2})$. The adjacent faces — now that S_5^1 has been excluded — can be

$(\sqrt{2}, \sqrt{2}, 1)$ of S_5^2,
$(\sqrt{2}, \sqrt{2}, 1)$ „ Cr_5^2.

Anyhow, the vertices $\sqrt{2}$ are triangular and consequently the reduced face polyhedron is a tetrahedron bounded by one $(\sqrt{2}, \sqrt{2}, \sqrt{2})$ and three $(\sqrt{2}, \sqrt{2}, 1)$. Only one of the latter triangles corresponds to Cr_5^2, the two remaining ones to S_5^2.

Although we can construct this tetrahedron, this case must be rejected. For the ordinary face polyhedron would require the following four triangles, whose edges are equal to

$\sqrt{2}$, $\sqrt{2}$ and $\sqrt{2}$, corresponding to ($\sqrt{2}$, $\sqrt{2}$, 1) of Cr_5^2,
$\sqrt{2}$, $\sqrt{2}$ „ 1, „ „ ($\sqrt{2}$, $\sqrt{2}$, $\sqrt{2}$) „ Cr_5^2,
$\sqrt{2}$, $\sqrt{2}$ „ 1, „ „ ($\sqrt{2}$, $\sqrt{2}$, 1) „ S_5^2,
$\sqrt{2}$, $\sqrt{2}$ „ 1, „ „ ($\sqrt{2}$, $\sqrt{2}$, 1) „ S_5^2,

and this cannot be realized.

In order to prove that S_5^2 is to be rejected we consider the triangle ($\sqrt{2}$, $\sqrt{2}$, 1). Now that S_5^1 and Cr_5^1 have been excluded we can only admit as adjacent faces the same triangles, and as the vertices $\sqrt{2}$ must be triangular we are led to a tetrahedron bounded by these triangles only. This cannot be realized.

Discussion. § 43. The edge polyhedra of the remaining polytopes S_5, Cr_5 and HM_5 have equal edges. We will henceforth consider the ordinary face polyhedra, and their faces will be indicated, as in the preceding chapter, by means of the length of their edges. Hence

S_5 is represented by triangle (1, 1, 1) with the angles α,
Cr_5 „ „ „ square (1, 1, 1, 1) „ „ „ β,
HM_5 „ „ „ triangle ($\sqrt{2}$, $\sqrt{2}$, 1) „ „ „ δ, δ and γ.

Let HM_5 bound a semiregular polytope. The vertices of ($\sqrt{2}$, $\sqrt{2}$, 1) are triangular and thus the face polyhedron is a tetrahedron. The adjacent face at an edge $\sqrt{2}$ is an other triangle ($\sqrt{2}$, $\sqrt{2}$, 1). Now we are led to two different cases:

1⁰. The face polyhedron is bounded by one (1, 1, 1) and three ($\sqrt{2}$, $\sqrt{2}$, 1).

2⁰. The face polyhedron is bounded by four ($\sqrt{2}$, $\sqrt{2}$, 1).

1⁰. The corresponding vertex polytope is S_5^1 (art. 31, B), whence

$$R_1 = \frac{15}{2} R_0, \; R_2 = 20 R_0, \; R_3 = (5 + 15) R_0, R_4 = \left(6 + \frac{15}{8}\right) R_0,$$
$$R_5 = \left(1 + \frac{3}{8}\right) R_0.$$

We will describe the polytope and determine R_0 in the following pages.

2^0. The corresponding vertex polytope is $S_5{}^2$ (art. 30), whence

$$R_1 = 10 R_0, \quad R_2 = 30 R_0, \quad R_3 = 30 R_0, \quad R_4 = \left(6 + \frac{15}{4}\right) R_0,$$
$$R_5 = \frac{3}{4} R_0.$$

The polytope will be investigated more closely later on.

We cannot bound a polytope by means of Cr_5 only, for 3β exceeds $360°$.

The simplest combination of Cr_5 and HM_5 leads to a face polyhedron bounded by one (1, 1, 1, 1) and four ($\sqrt{2}, \sqrt{2}$, 1). And this is a space filling.

There is no semiregular polytope bounded by S_5 only. For the vertices of the face polyhedron are 3- or 4-angular. Hence we are confined to T, a 3-angular bipyramid and O. Now T and O lead to the regular S_6 and Cr_6 respectively and the bipyramid does not admit a circumscribed sphere.

We can combine Cr_5 and S_5. The vertices of the square corresponding to Cr_5 are triangular. We can make to pass through such a vertex, besides that square, two triangles or an other square and a triangle. In the former case there results a 4-angular pyramid (art. 31, A, C) and we showed in the preceding chapter that no fivedimensional polytope corresponds to it. In the latter case we are led to P_3 and hence to the vertex polytope HM_5. So

$$R_1 = 8 R_0, \; R_2 = \frac{80}{3} R_0, \; R_3 = 40 R_0, \; R_4 = 24 R_0, \; R_5 = \left(\frac{8}{3} + 1\right) R_0.$$

So we will have to consider the following cases more closely:

$$\left.\begin{array}{llll} \text{A.} \; . \; . \; . & S_5^2 & \text{is vertex} & \text{polytope} \\ \text{B.} \; . \; . \; . & S_5^1 & \text{,,} & \text{,,} \\ \text{C.} \; . \; . \; . & HM_5 & \text{,,} & \text{,,} \end{array}\right\} .$$

(72, 720, 2160, 2160, 702, 54). § 44. Case **A.** S_5^2 is vertex polytope.

The following list where

$$a = \frac{1}{4}\sqrt{2},\ b = \frac{1}{10}\sqrt{10},\ c = \frac{3}{20}\sqrt{10},\ d = \frac{1}{10}\sqrt{15}$$

contains the coordinates of the vertices of S_5^2 with respect to a rectangular system of axes. The origin is the centre of S_5^2. The axis X_5 joins the centres of two parallel tC_5, the axis X_4 is parallel to the line that joins, in one of these tC_5, the centre of a T to that of the O opposite to it, while the axes X_1, X_2 and X_3 are parallel to the vertex axes of that O.

$$\left.\begin{array}{rrrrr} 2a, & 0, & 0, & -b, & d \\ -2a, & 0, & 0, & -b, & d \\ 0, & 2a, & 0, & -b, & d \\ 0, & -2a, & 0, & -b, & d \\ 0, & 0, & 2a, & -b, & d \\ 0, & 0, & -2a, & -b, & d \end{array}\right\}, \quad \left.\begin{array}{rrrrr} a, & a, & a, & c, & d \\ a, & -a, & -a, & c, & d \\ -a, & a, & -a, & c, & d \\ -a, & -a, & a, & c, & d \end{array}\right\},$$

$$\left.\begin{array}{rrrrr} -a, & a, & a, & -c, & -d \\ a, & -a, & a, & -c, & -d \\ a, & a, & -a, & -c, & -d \\ -a, & -a, & -a, & -c, & -d \end{array}\right\}, \quad \left.\begin{array}{rrrrr} 2a, & 0, & 0, & b, & -d \\ -2a, & 0, & 0, & b, & -d \\ 0, & 2a, & 0, & b, & -d \\ 0, & -2a, & 0, & b, & -d \\ 0, & 0, & 2a, & b, & -d \\ 0, & 0, & -2a, & b, & -d \end{array}\right\}.$$

These four sets of vertices represent 2O and 2T. We will abbreviate them in this way:

$$\begin{array}{l} O(\ 2a, 0, 0, -b,\ \ d),\ T(\ a, a, a, c,\ \ d), \\ T(-a, a, a, -c, -d),\ O(2a, 0, 0, b, -d). \end{array} \quad . \; . \; . \quad (a)$$

In order to investigate the polytope we will introduce a system of six axes, whose origin is the centre of the polytope.

The axis X_6 is perpendicular to a vertex polytope, five axes are parallel to those mentioned above.

As the circumscribed radius of S_5^2 is $\frac{1}{2}\sqrt{3}$, that of the polytope is 1, and the centre of S_5^2 is at a distance $\frac{1}{2}$ from the origin. So we have, for the present, the following 21 vertices:

$$(0;\ 0,\ 0,\ 0,\ 0,\ 1),$$

$$\left.\begin{array}{l} O(\ 2a, 0, 0, -b, \quad d, \tfrac{1}{2}),\ T(\ a,\ a,\ a,\ c, \quad d, \tfrac{1}{2}), \\ T(-a, a, a, -c, -d, \tfrac{1}{2}),\ O(2a,\ 0,\ 0,\ b, -d, \tfrac{1}{2}), \end{array}\right\} \quad . \quad (b).$$

We will now determine the vertex polytopes which correspond to the vertices of (a). We will begin at

$$a,\ a,\ a,\ c,\ d,\ \tfrac{1}{2}.$$

Its centre is

$$\tfrac{1}{2}a,\ \tfrac{1}{2}a,\ \tfrac{1}{2}a,\ \tfrac{1}{2}c,\ \tfrac{1}{2}d,\ \tfrac{1}{4}.$$

As the vertex polytope of a S_5^2 is the prismotope (9, 18, 15, 6), 9 vertices of the required vertex polytope are contained in (b) viz.

$$\left.\begin{array}{l} 2a,\ 0,\ 0, -b, d, \tfrac{1}{2} \\ 0, 2a,\ 0, -b, d, \tfrac{1}{2} \\ 0,\ 0, 2a, -b, d, \tfrac{1}{2} \end{array}\right\},\quad \left.\begin{array}{l} a, -a, -a, c, d, \tfrac{1}{2} \\ -a,\ a, -a, c, d, \tfrac{1}{2} \\ -a, -a,\ a, c, d, \tfrac{1}{2} \end{array}\right\},\quad \left.\begin{array}{l} 2a,\ 0,\ 0, b, -d, \tfrac{1}{2} \\ 0, 2a,\ 0, b, -d, \tfrac{1}{2} \\ 0,\ 0, 2a, b, -d, \tfrac{1}{2} \end{array}\right\}.$$

Besides

$$0,\ 0,\ 0,\ 0,\ 0,\ 1$$

belongs to that vertex polytope.

The 10 remaining vertices are diametrically opposite to them

$$a,\ a,\ a,\ c,\ d,\ -\tfrac{1}{2},$$

$$\left.\begin{array}{l} -a,\ a,\ a, \tfrac{5}{3}c, 0, 0 \\ a, -a,\ a, \tfrac{5}{3}c, 0, 0 \\ a,\ a, -a, \tfrac{5}{3}c, 0, 0 \end{array}\right\},\quad \left.\begin{array}{l} 0, 2a, 2a, 0, 0, 0 \\ 2a,\ 0, 2a, 0, 0, 0 \\ 2a, 2a,\ 0, 0, 0, 0 \end{array}\right\},\quad \left.\begin{array}{l} -a,\ a,\ a, \frac{c}{3}, 2d, 0 \\ a, -a,\ a, \frac{c}{3}, 2d, 0 \\ a,\ a, -a, \frac{c}{3}, 2d, 0 \end{array}\right\}.$$

By determining, in the same way, the vertex polytope for

$$2a,\ 0,\ 0,\ -b,\ d,\ \tfrac{1}{2}$$

we get

$$2a,\ 0,\ 0,\ -b,\ d,\ -\tfrac{1}{2},$$

$$\left.\begin{matrix} 2a, -2a, & 0, & 0,0,0 \\ 2a, & 0,-2a, & 0,0,0 \\ a,- & a,- & a,\tfrac{5}{3}c,0,0 \end{matrix}\right\},\ \left.\begin{matrix} 2a, & 0,2a, & 0,0,0 \\ 2a,2a, & 0, & 0,0,0 \\ a, & a, & a,-\tfrac{5}{3}c,0,0 \end{matrix}\right\},\ \left.\begin{matrix} a, & a,-a, & \frac{c}{3}, 2d,0 \\ a,-a, & a, & \frac{c}{3}, 2d,0 \\ 0, & 0, & 0,-2b, 2d,0 \end{matrix}\right\}.$$

The other vertices of (a) differ only in the signs of the coordinates. So we can easily deduce their vertex polytopes. The following list contains all the new vertices.

$$\left.\begin{matrix} 0,0,0,-2b,\ 2d,\ 0, & 0,0,0,\ \ 2b,-2d,0) \\ T(-a,a,a,\ \tfrac{5}{3}c,\ 0,0), & T(a,a,a,-\tfrac{5}{3}c,\ \ 0,0) \\ & [2a,2a,0],0,0,\ 0, \\ T(-a,a,a,\ \frac{c}{3},\ 2d,0), & T(a,a,a,-\frac{c}{3},-2d,0). \end{matrix}\right\}\ (c)$$

Their number is 30. Moreover

$$\left.\begin{matrix} O(2a,0,0,-b,\ \ d,-\tfrac{1}{2}), & T(\ a,a,a,c,\ \ d,-\tfrac{1}{2}), \\ T(-a,a,a,-c,-d,-\tfrac{1}{2}), & O(2a,0,0,b,-d,-\tfrac{1}{2}). \end{matrix}\right\}\ .\ .\ (d)$$

This is a S_5^2 which is symmetrical to (a) with respect to the space $x_6 = 0$. It is obvious that the vertex polytopes of the vertices of (d) are those of the list (c) and

$$0,\ 0,\ 0,\ 0,\ 0,\ -1.$$

Probably the latter vertex completes the polytope. But before demonstrating it we will transform the coordinates by the following substitution:

$$x_4' = \quad 2dx_4 + 2bx_5,$$
$$x_5' = -2bx_4 + 2dx_5.$$

The following list contains the coordinates of the vertices for which $x_6 = 1$, $\tfrac{1}{2}$ and 0; here

$$e = \frac{1}{4}\sqrt{2}, \qquad k = \frac{1}{4}\sqrt{6}.$$

0, 0, 0, 0, 0, 1		$x_6=1$
O($2e$, 0, 0, 0, $\frac{1}{2}$, $\frac{1}{2}$) T(e, e, e, k, 0, $\frac{1}{2}$) T($-e$, e, e, $-k$, 0, $\frac{1}{2}$) O($2e$, 0, 0, 0, $-\frac{1}{2}$, $\frac{1}{2}$)		$x_6=\frac{1}{2}$
0, 0, 0, 0, 1, 0	$x_5=1$	
T($-e$, e, e, k, $\frac{1}{2}$, 0), T(e, e, e, $-k$, $\frac{1}{2}$, 0)	$x_5=\frac{1}{2}$	
[$2e$, $2e$, 0], 0, 0, 0	$x_5=0$	$x_6=0$
T($-e$, e, e, k, $-\frac{1}{2}$, 0), T(e, e, e, $-k$, $-\frac{1}{2}$, 0)	$x_5=-\frac{1}{2}$	
0, 0, 0, 0, -1, 0	$x_5=-1$	

Now we will determine the vertex polytope for

$$2e,\ 2e,\ 0,\ 0,\ 0,\ 0.$$

In order to show that it is a S_5^2 we will arrange its vertices like those of table (a).

$$\left\{\begin{array}{cccccc} e, & e, & e, & k, & 0, & \frac{1}{2} \\ e, & e, & -e, & -k, & 0, & \frac{1}{2} \\ 2e, & 0, & 0, & 0, & \frac{1}{2}, & \frac{1}{2} \\ 0, & 2e, & 0, & 0, & -\frac{1}{2}, & \frac{1}{2} \\ 2e, & 0, & 0, & 0, & -\frac{1}{2}, & \frac{1}{2} \\ 0, & 2e, & 0, & 0, & \frac{1}{2}, & \frac{1}{2} \end{array}\right\}, \quad \left\{\begin{array}{cccccc} 2e, & 0, & 2e, & 0, & 0, & 0 \\ 0, & 2e, & 2e, & 0, & 0, & 0 \\ e, & e, & e, & -k, & \frac{1}{2}, & 0 \\ e, & e, & e, & -k, & -\frac{1}{2}, & 0 \end{array}\right\},$$

$$\left\{\begin{array}{cccccc} 2e, & 0, & -2e, & 0, & 0, & 0 \\ 0, & 2e, & -2e, & 0, & 0, & 0 \\ e, & e, & -e, & k, & \frac{1}{2}, & 0 \\ e, & e, & -e, & k, & -\frac{1}{2}, & 0 \end{array}\right\}, \quad \left\{\begin{array}{cccccc} e, & e, & e, & k, & 0, & -\frac{1}{2} \\ e, & e, & -e, & -k, & 0, & -\frac{1}{2} \\ 2e, & 0, & 0, & 0, & \frac{1}{2}, & -\frac{1}{2} \\ 0, & 2e, & 0, & 0, & -\frac{1}{2}, & -\frac{1}{2} \\ 2e, & 0, & 0, & 0, & -\frac{1}{2}, & -\frac{1}{2} \\ 0, & 2e, & 0, & 0, & -\frac{1}{2}, & -\frac{1}{2} \end{array}\right\}.$$

So we have demonstrated that the vertex polytope is S_5^2 for any vertex. Then we know that

$$R_0 = 1 + 20 + 30 + 20 + 1 = 72,$$

whence

$R_1 = 720$, $R_2 = 2160$, $R_3 = 2160$, $R_4 = 432 + 270$, $R_5 = 54$.

As the vertex polytope shows 3 characteristics of regularity, *the degree of regularity of the polytope is* $\frac{4}{6}$.

There are two kinds of R_4 viz. 432 C_5 and 270 C_{16}. Through a bounding T pass $2C_{16}$ and 1 C_5 and 3 HM_5.

(32, 240, 640, 640, 252, 44). § 45. Case **B**. S_5^1 is vertex polytope.

This case represents HM_6. We may consider the derivation of HM_n from M_n as a truncation at the alternating vertices. Then the truncated spaces are HM_{n-1}, the truncating ones the vertex polytopes of M_n i. e. S_{n-1}. In our case we obtain 32 S_5 and 12 HM_5.

The vertices are represented by

$$\} + + + + + + \{$$

(art. 35). Their number is 32.

It is sufficient to show that the vertex polytope is S_5^1 for any vertex. We obtain its vertices by changing in the given symbol *pairs* of signs. Their number is consequently $(6)_2 = 15$. The subjoined scheme represents the vertices of the vertex polytope for

$$+ + + + + +.$$

The arrangement shows a bounding C_5 and its opposite tC_5.

$--++++$, $+--+++$, $+-+-++$, $+-++-+$, $+-+++-$
$-+-+++$, $++--++$, $++-+-+$, $++-++-$,
$-++-++$, $++++--$, $+++-+-$, $+++--+$,
$-+++-+$,
$-++++-$.

So the limits are:

$$R_0 = 32, \quad R_1 = 240, \quad R_2 = 640, \quad R_3 = 160 + 480,$$
$$R_4 = 192 + 60, \quad R_5 = 32 + 12.$$

The R_0, R_1 and R_2 are equal. The R_3 are T, but through any of the 160 pass 3 HM_5 (3 C_{16}), through any of the 480 pass 2 HM_5 and 1 S_5 (2 C_5 and 1 C_{16}). Thus *the degree of regularity is* $\frac{3\frac{1}{2}}{6} = \frac{7}{12}$.

Any C_{16} is situated between 2 HM_5, any C_5 between a HM_5 and a S_5.

(27, 216, 720, 080, 648, 99). § 46. Case **C**. HM_5 is vertex polytope.

The circumscribed radius of HM_5 being $\frac{\sqrt{6}}{3}$, its distance from the centre of the polytope is $\frac{\sqrt{6}}{12}$ and the circumscribed radius of the polytope is $\frac{\sqrt{6}}{3}$. Hence we can represent one vertex by

$$0, 0, 0, 0, 0, 4b, \qquad \left(b = \frac{\sqrt{6}}{12}\right)$$

and the vertices of the corresponding vertex polytope by

$$\}a, a, a, a, a\{, b. \qquad \left(a = \frac{\sqrt{2}}{4}\right)$$

We now determine the vertex polytope for one of these vertices, e. g. for

$$a, a, a, a, a, b \quad \ldots\ldots \quad (1)$$

We obtained already

$$0, 0, 0, 0, 0, 4b$$

and those 10 which we derive from (1) by changing the signs of two a.

The centre of the vertex polytope is

$$\tfrac{1}{4}a, \tfrac{1}{4}a, \tfrac{1}{4}a, \tfrac{1}{4}a, \tfrac{1}{4}a, \tfrac{1}{4}b.$$

Opposite to any of its vertices a C_5 is situated, the centre of which is at a distance $\frac{3}{20}\sqrt{10}$ from the centre of the polytope. The centre of the one opposite to

$$-a, -a, a, a, a, b$$

is

$$a, a, -\frac{a}{5}, -\frac{a}{5}, -\frac{a}{5}, -\frac{b}{5}.$$

Three of its vertices appear among those mentioned above viz.

$$\begin{array}{llllll} a, & a, & -a, & -a, & a, & b, \\ a, & a, & -a, & a, & -a, & b, \\ a, & a, & a, & -a, & -a, & b, \end{array}$$

The remaining two are

$$2a, 0, 0, 0, 0, -2b, \qquad 0, 2a, 0, 0, 0, -2b.$$

So we get two new vertices of the polytope. It is obvious that the three remaining vertices of the vertex polytope can be obtained by putting $2a$ at the 3^d^ 4th and 5th place.

The vertex polytopes for the other vertices lead to an other set of five new vertices which differ from the preceding ones in the sign of the $2a$.

Now it appears that the vertex polytopes of these ten new vertices do not give rise to new vertices and hence that the polytope is complete with these 27 vertices [1]).

The following table, which contains the vertices of the vertex polytope of

$$2a, 0, 0, 0, 0, -2b,$$

shows that this vertex polytope is a HM_5.

$$\left.\begin{array}{llllll} 0, & 2a, & 0, & 0, & 0, & -2b \\ 0, & 0, & 2a, & 0, & 0, & -2b \\ 0, & 0, & 0, & 2a, & 0, & -2b \\ 0, & 0, & 0, & 0, & 2a, & -2b \end{array}\right\}, \qquad \left.\begin{array}{llllll} 0, & -2a, & 0, & 0, & 0, & -2b \\ 0, & 0, & -2a, & 0, & 0, & -2b \\ 0, & 0, & 0, & -2a, & 0, & -2b \\ 0, & 0, & 0, & 0, & -2a, & -2b \end{array}\right\},$$

---

[1]) The remarkable property of this polytope to admit only one kind of diagonals equal to $\sqrt{2}$ times an edge has induced Dr. SCHOUTE to point out an analogy between the 27 vertices of this polytope each of which admits 16 adjacent vertices and the 27 straight lines of a cubic surface each of which is crossed by 16 other ones. See *Proceedings* of Amsterdam, vol. XIII, p. 375.

$$\left.\begin{array}{llllll} a, & a, & a, & a, & a, & b, \\ a, & -a, & & -a, & a, & a, \; b, \\ a, & -a, & a, & -a, & a, & b, \\ a, & -a, & a, & a, & -a, & b, \end{array}\right\}, \quad \left.\begin{array}{llllll} a, & -a, & -a, & -a, & -a, & b, \\ a, & a, & a, & -a, & -a, & b, \\ a, & a, & -a, & a, & -a, & b, \\ a, & a, & -a, & -a, & a, & b. \end{array}\right\}.$$

So we find

$$R_0 = 27, \; R_1 = 216, \; R_2 = 720, \; R_3 = 1080, \; R_4 = 216 + 432$$
$$R_5 = 72 + 27.$$

The R_0, R_1, R_2 and R_3 are equal. The R_4 are C_5, and are divided into two kinds whose numbers are 216 and 432 respectively. Those of the former kind are situated between a S_5 and a Cr_5, those of the latter kind between 2 Cr_5. The polytope is bounded by 72 S_5 and 27 Cr_5.

The degree of regularity is $\frac{4\frac{1}{2}}{6} = \frac{3}{4}$.

CHAPTER VI.

SEVENDIMENSIONAL SEMIREGULAR POLYTOPES.

Preliminary. § 47. We will now determine the sevendimensional polytopes the degree of regularity of which is at least $\frac{1}{2}$. Their vertices, edges and faces must be equal, their spaces at least half equal. The following list, to which we will refer in the course of the investigation, contains the dihedral angles at the bounding R_4 and the solid angles round the bounding R_3 of S_6, Cr_6 and the polytopes of the preceding chapter. In the first column V_{27} represents the polytope described in art. 46, V_{72} that of art. 44. In the second column, the indices S_4 and Cr_4 are to indicate the pairs of HM_5 that have a S_4 and those that have a Cr_4 in common.

	Dihedral angles	Solid angles round R_3
S_6	$80° 24' 21'' = \alpha$	$61° 13' 3''$
Cr_6	$131° 48' 36'' = \beta$	$167° 14' 24''$
HM_6	$(HM_5, HM_5) = 90° = \gamma$	$(HM_5, HM_5, HM_5) = 90°$
	$(S_5, HM_5) = 114° 5' 42'' = \delta$	$(S_5, HM_5, HM_5) = 138° 11' 24''$
V_{27}	$(Cr_5, Cr_5) = 104° 28\ 39'' = \varphi$	$180°$
	$(Cr_5, S_5) = 127° 45' 40'' = \psi$	
V_{72}	$(HM_5, HM_5)_{S_4} = 104° 28' 39'' = \varphi$	
	$(HM_5, HM_5)_{Cr_4} = 120° = \chi$	

Reduced space polygons.

§ 48. We will introduce again into the present discussion the *reduced space polygons* of the sixdimensional polytopes and the *reduced space polyhedra* of the sevendimensional ones. The former do not differ from the space polygons in the case of S_6, Cr_6 and V_{27}.

The following list contains the reduced space polygons, viz. the lengths of the edges of the face polytope through their vertices, the dihedral angles which correspond to their angles, the bounding R_4 which correspond to their vertices and the bounding R_5 which correspond to their edges.

	Edges through vertices.	Corresponding angles.	R_4 corresponding to vertices.	R_5 corresponding to edges.
S_6	1, 1, 1,	α, α, α	S_4, S_4, S_4	S_5, S_5, S_5
Cr_6	1, 1, 1, 1	$\beta, \beta, \beta, \beta$	S_4, S_4, S_4, S_4	S_5, S_5, S_5, S_5
HM_6	$\sqrt{2}, \sqrt{2}, \sqrt{2}$	γ, γ, γ	Cr_4, Cr_4, Cr_4	HM_5, HM_5, HM_5
	$\sqrt{2}$, 1, 1	γ, δ, δ	Cr_4, S_4, S_4	S_5, HM_5, HM_5
V_{27}	1, 1, 1	φ, ψ, ψ	S_4, S_4, S_4	S_5, Cr_5, Cr_5
V_{72}	1, $\sqrt{2}$, $\sqrt{2}$	φ, χ, χ	S_4, Cr_4, Cr_4	HM_5, HM_5, HM_5

Discussion.

§ 49. It is impossible to bound a semiregular polytope by means of S_6 only. In fact the vertices of a space polyhedron are 3- or 4-angular. Hence we are confined to T, O and the 3-angular bipyramid. We showed in art. 43 that these must be excluded. We have yet still to consider the case in which the polytope is bounded by more than one kind of limiting polytopes. So we must consider the possibility of more than one kind of space polyhedra. But as the face polytope admits a circumscribed spherical space and as its edges are equally long the circumradii of the different space polyhedra must be equal.

We cannot limit a polytope by Cr_6 only, 3β exceeding 360°.

We can combine S_6 and Cr_6. If the polytope is bounded

by equal spaces we are led, by the reasoning of art. 43 to the space polyhedron P_8 and hence to the vertex polytope V_{27}. We will have to consider this case more closely.

The case of different space polyhedra must be rejected for the reason that has been given higher up.

It is impossible to bound a polytope by V_{27} only, the solid angle being 180°.

Nor can we bound a polytope by V_{72} only. We can admit only a tetrahedron as space polyhedron and this can not be limited by triangles $(\sqrt{2}, \sqrt{2}, 1)$.

Nor can we construct the tetrahedron which would be required for HM_6.

We will now examine the possibility of combining V_{27} with an other polytope. In the space polyhedron V_{27} is represented by the triangle $(1, 1, 1)$ (φ, ψ, ψ). The vertex at ψ is triangular whence we are led to a tetrahedron. The adjacent sides of φ corresponding to Cr_5, the adjacent faces at these sides correspond necessarily to other V_{27}. Hence the fourth face corresponds to S_6. So the space polyhedron is a tetrahedron bounded by 3 triangles $(\sqrt{2}, \sqrt{2}, 1)$ and 1 triangle $(1, 1, 1)$. This leads (art. 43) to the edge polytope S^1_5, and hence to the vertex polytope HM_6 (art. 45).

We will now try to combine V_{72} with an other polytope. In the reduced space polyhedron V_{72} is represented by

$$(1, \sqrt{2}, \sqrt{2}) \quad (\varphi, \chi, \chi),$$

the vertex 1 corresponding to S_4, the vertex $\sqrt{2}$ to Cr_4 and any of the edges to HM_5. We can only admit a tetrahedron as space polyhedron, the vertices $\sqrt{2}$ being 3-angular. Now the fourth vertex may be 1 or $\sqrt{2}$. Both cases lead to a combination with HM_6 In the former case the triangle $(\sqrt{2}, \sqrt{2}, \sqrt{2})$, in the latter case the triangle $(\sqrt{2}, 1, 1)$ is lacking. So we are forced to admit two kinds of space tetrahedra viz. $(1, 1, \sqrt{2}, \sqrt{2})$ $(V_{72}, V_{72}, HM_6, HM_6)$ and $(1, \sqrt{2}, \sqrt{2}, \sqrt{2})$ $(HM_6, V_{72}, V_{72}, V_{72})$.

The corresponding space tetrahedra admit the edges

$$(1, 1)\ (\sqrt{2}, \sqrt{2})\ (\sqrt{2}, \sqrt{2}), \quad . \quad . \quad . \quad . \quad (a)$$

$$(\sqrt{2}, 1)\ (\sqrt{2}, 1)\ (\sqrt{2}, 1), \quad . \quad . \quad . \quad . \quad (b)$$

where any couple of edges between ( ) are opposite to each other. This combination can be realized in a face polytope bounded by three (*a*) and two (*b*).

For the corresponding edge polytope we find

$$R_1 = \frac{3}{2} R_0 + R_0,\ R_2 = \frac{4}{3} R_0 + \frac{3}{2} R_0,\ R_3 = \frac{1}{4} R_0 + \frac{3}{2} R_0,$$

$$R_4 = \frac{1}{4} R_0 + \frac{1}{3} R_0,$$

whence by EULER's theorem

$$R_0 = 12,\ R_1 = 18 + 12,\ R_2 = 16p_3 + 18p_4,\ R_3 = 3T + 18P_3,$$

$$R_4 = 3P_T + 4PT_3,$$

where PT_3 represents a prismotope the auxiliary polygons of which are triangles.

Let x represent the number of vertices of the vertex polytope, y that of the polytope; then we find for the vertex polytope

$$R_0 = x,\ R_1 = 6x,\ R_2 = (6+4)x,\ R_3 = (4+3)x,$$

$$R_4 = \left(\frac{3}{5} + \frac{9}{5}\right)x,\ R_5 = \left(\frac{1}{5} + \frac{1}{5}\right)x,$$

and for the polytope itself

$$R_0 = y,\ R_1 = \frac{xy}{2},\ R_2 = 2xy,\ R_3 = \left(\frac{3}{2} + 1\right)xy,\ R_4 = \left(\frac{4}{5} + \frac{3}{8}\right)xy,$$

$$R_5 = \left(\frac{1}{10} + \frac{9}{80}\right)xy,\ R_6 = \left(\frac{1}{160} + \frac{1}{360}\right)xy,$$

whence by EULER's theorem

$$y\left(1 - \frac{41}{1440}x\right) = 2.$$

We have necessarily

$$\frac{41}{1440}x < 1,$$

$$x < 36.$$

Besides, x must be a multiple of 5 and only $x = 35$ leads to an integer y, whence $y = 576$. Thus we find for the vertex polytope

$$R_0 = 35, \ R_1 = 210, \ R_2 = 210 + 140, \ R_3 = 140T + 150\,O,$$
$$R_4 = 21C_5 + 63tC_5, \ R_5 = 7S_5^1 + 7S_5^2.$$

This is S_6^2 or S_6^3.

So we have to consider:

A. V_{27} is vertex polytope.

B. HM_6 „ „ „

C. S_6^2 „ „ „

(56, 756, 4032, 10080, 12096, 6048, 702). § 50. Case **A**. V_{27} is vertex polytope.

$$R_0 = 56, \ R_1 = 756, \ R_2 = 4032, \ R_3 = 10080, \ R_4 = 12096,$$
$$R_5 = (2016 + 4032)S_5, \ R_6 = 576\,S_6 + 126\,Cr_6.$$

There are two kinds of bounding S_5. Any of the 2016 S_5 is situated between a S_6 and a Cr_6, any of the 4032 S_5 between two Cr_6.

The degree of regularity is $\frac{5\frac{1}{2}}{7} = \frac{11}{14}$.

Circumradius $= \frac{1}{2}\sqrt{3}$.

We can represent one of its vertices by

$$0,\ 0,\ 0,\ 0,\ 0, \quad 0,\ 3c\ (1), \quad \left(c = \frac{1}{6}\sqrt{3}\right)$$

and hence the corresponding vertex polytope (art. 46) by

$$0,\ 0,\ 0,\ 0,\ 0, \quad 4b,\ \ c\ (2), \quad \left(b = \frac{1}{12}\sqrt{6}\right)$$
$$\{\,a,\ a,\ a,\ a,\ a\,\}, \quad b,\ \ c\ (3), \quad \left(a = \frac{1}{4}\sqrt{2}\right)$$
$$[2a,\ 0,\ 0,\ 0,\ 0],\ -2b,\ \ c\ (4).$$

We will now determine the vertex polytope corresponding to

$$0,\ 0,\ 0,\ 0,\ 0,\ 4b,\ c.$$

Its centre is

$$0,\ 0,\ 0,\ 0,\ 0,\ \frac{4}{3}b,\ \frac{1}{3}c.$$

To that vertex polytope belong (1) and (3) to the number

of 17. We have yet to determine the Cr_5 opposite to (1). Its centre is

$$0,\ 0,\ 0,\ 0,\ 0,\ 2b,\ -c,$$

and it is obvious that we may ascertain

$$[2a,\ 0,\ 0,\ 0,\ 0],\ 2b-c \quad . \quad . \quad . \quad . \quad . \quad (5)$$

In fact the vertices of this Cr_5 are at a distance 1 from (2) and at a distance $\sqrt{2}$ from (1).

Hence the origin is centre of symmetry. So we derive from (3), (2) and (1)

$$\{-a,\ a,\ a,\ a,\ a\},\ -b,\ -c \quad . \quad . \quad . \quad . \quad (6)$$

$$0,\ 0,\ 0,\ 0,\ 0,\ -4b,\ -c \quad . \quad . \quad . \quad . \quad (7)$$

$$0,\ 0,\ 0,\ 0,\ 0,\quad 0,\ -3c \quad . \quad . \quad . \quad . \quad (8)$$

(126, 2016, …080, 20160, …6128, 4788, 632). § 51. Case **B**. HM_6 is vertex polytope.

$$R_0 = 126,\quad R_1 = 2016,\quad R_2 = 10080,\quad R_3 = 20160,$$

$$R_4 = (4032 + 12096)\,C_5,\quad R_5 = 4032\,S_5 + 756\,Cr_5,$$

$$R_6 = 576\,S_6 + 56 V_{27}.$$

Through any of the 4032 C_5 pass 3 V_{27} (and 3 Cr_5), through any of the 12096 C_5 pass 2 S_6 and 1 V_{27} (2 S_5 and 1 Cr_5).

The degree of regularity is $\dfrac{4\frac{1}{2}}{7} = \dfrac{9}{14}$.

Circumradius $= 1$.

We represent one vertex by

$$0,\ 0,\ 0,\ 0,\ 0,\ 0,\ 1 \quad . \quad . \quad . \quad . \quad . \quad . \quad (1)$$

and the corresponding vertex polytope by

$$\{a,\ a,\ a,\ a,\ a,\ a\},\ \tfrac{1}{2} \quad . \quad . \quad (2) \qquad \left(a = \frac{1}{4}\sqrt{2}\right)$$

We will now determine the vertex polytope corresponding to one of the vertices (2), namely

$$a,\ a,\ a,\ a,\ a,\ a,\ \tfrac{1}{2},$$

to which belong (1) and those derived from (2) by changing two signs, in the whole 16 vertices. The centre is

$$\tfrac{1}{2}a,\ \tfrac{1}{2}a,\ \tfrac{1}{2}a,\ \tfrac{1}{2}a,\ \tfrac{1}{2}a,\ \tfrac{1}{2}a,\ \tfrac{1}{4}$$

and the vertices are situated symmetrically with respect to

that centre. Hence it is easy to determine the lacking vertices, viz.

$$a,\ a,\ a,\ a,\ a,\ a,\ -\tfrac{1}{2}$$

and those derived from

$$2a,\ 2a,\ 0,\ 0,\ 0,\ 0,\quad 0,$$

by the permutations of $2a$ in the first 6 places.

The new vertices, derived in the same manner from all the vertices (2), are

$$[2a,\ 2a,\ 0,\ 0,\ 0,\ 0],\ 0,$$

to the number of 60. Hence the origin is centre of symmetry. So the vertices are contained in

2	$0,\ 0,\ 0,\ 0,\ 0,\ 0,\ \pm 1$
64	$\{a,\ a,\ a,\ a,\ a,\ a\},\ \pm \tfrac{1}{2}$
60	$[2a,\ 2a,\ 0,\ 0,\ 0,\ 0],\ 0.$

(576, 10080, § 52. Case **C**. S_6^2 is vertex polytope.

40320, 50400, 23688, 4284, 182. $R_0 = 576,\ R_1 = 10080,\ R_2 = 40320,\ R_3 = 30240 + 20160,$

$$R_4 = 16128\,C_5 + 7560\,C_{16},\quad R_5 = 2016\,S_5 + 2268\,HM_5,$$

$$R_6 = 126\,HM_6 + 56\,V_{72}.$$

Its degree of regularity is $\dfrac{3\frac{1}{2}}{7} = \dfrac{1}{2}$.

The circumradius is $= \dfrac{1}{2}\sqrt{7}$, that of S_6^2 being $= \sqrt{\dfrac{6}{7}}$.

Hence we can represent a bounding HM_6 by

$$\{a,\ a,\ a,\ a,\ a,\ a\},\ 1\quad \ldots\ (1)\qquad \left(a = \frac{1}{4}\sqrt{2}\right)$$

Let us determine the vertex polytope corresponding to

$$a,\ a,\ a,\ a,\ a,\ a,\ 1.$$

Its centre is

$$\tfrac{5}{7}a,\ \tfrac{5}{7}a,\ \tfrac{5}{7}a,\ \tfrac{5}{7}a,\ \tfrac{5}{7}a,\ \tfrac{5}{7}a,\ \tfrac{5}{7}.$$

We find 15 vertices included in (1) viz. those having two negative signs. They limit a truncating S_5^1 which bounds S_6^2. Let $A_1,\ A_2 \ldots,\ A_7$ be the vertices of S_6 from which the vertex polytope is derived and let that S_5^1 truncate S_6 at A_7.

Its centre is

$$\tfrac{1}{3}a,\ \tfrac{1}{3}a,\ \tfrac{1}{3}a,\ \tfrac{1}{3}a,\ \tfrac{1}{3}a,\ \tfrac{1}{3}a,\ 1.$$

Hence A_7 is represented by

$$-a,\ -a,\ -a,\ -a,\ -a,\ -a,\ +2.$$

Hence we derive the 20 vertices of the truncated S_5^2. They are

$$(2a,\ 2a,\ 2a,\ 0,\ 0,\ 0),\ \tfrac{1}{2}.$$

So the vertices that result from the vertex polytopes of all the (1) are

$$[2a,\ 2a,\ 2a,\ 0,\ 0,\ 0],\ \tfrac{1}{2}\ .\ .\ .\ .\ .\ \quad (2)$$

Their number is 160.

In the same way we derive from (2) the following new vertices

$$\{-3a,\ a,\ a,\ a,\ a,\ a\},\ 0\ .\ .\ .\ .\ .\ \quad (3)$$

Their number is 192.

We infer from the symbol (3) that the vertices are situated symmetrically with respect to the origin. Hence the vertices are:

$$64\ .\ .\ .\ .\ .\ \{a,\ a,\ a,\ a,\ a,\ a\},\ \pm 1,$$
$$320\ .\ .\ .\ .\ .\ [2a,\ 2a,\ 2a,\ 0,\ 0,\ 0],\ \pm \tfrac{1}{2},$$
$$192\ .\ .\ .\ .\ \{-3a,\ a,\ a,\ a,\ a,\ a\},\ 0.$$

CHAPTER VII.

EIGHTDIMENSIONAL SEMIREGULAR POLYTOPES. CONCLUSION.

Preliminary. § 53. The 8-dimensional polytope whose degree of regularity is at least $\frac{1}{2}$ has equal vertices, edges, faces and limiting bodies. The following list contains the dihedral angles at a bounding R_5 and the solid angles round a bounding R_4 of S_7, Cr_7 and the polytopes described in the preceding chapter, V_{56}, V_{126} and V_{576} denoting the polytopes of art. 50, 51 and 52 respectively.

	Dihedral angles	Solid angles
S_7	$81°47'12 = \alpha$	$65°21'36''$
Cr_7	$135°35'5'' = \beta$	$182°20'20''$
V_{56}	$(Cr_6, Cr_6) = 120° = \gamma$	$218°12'48''$
	$(S_6, Cr_6) = 139°6'24'' = \delta$	
V_{126}	$(V_{27}, V_{27}) = 109°28'16'' = \varepsilon$	$(V_{27}, V_{27}, V_{27}) = 148°24'48''$
	$(S_6, V_{27}) = 130°53'36'' = \eta$	$(S_6, V_{27}, V_{27}) = 191°15'28''$
V_{576}	$(V_{72}, HM_6) = 125°15'52'' = \varphi$	$(V_{72}, V_{72}, V_{72}) = 148°24'48''$
	$(V_{72}, V_{72}) = \varepsilon$	$(HM_6, HM_6, V_{72}) = 190°31'44''$
	$(HM_6, HM_6) = \gamma$	$(V_{72}, V_{72}, HM_6) = 180°$

Exclusion of V_{576}. § 54. We cannot combine V_{576} with any of the polytopes of the preceding chapter, its bounding polytopes being V_{72} and HM_6.

Let us endeavour to construct a polytope by means of

V_{576} only. Through a bounding S_5 of V_{576} pass 2 HM_6, which include an angle of 120°. Hence, in the polytope bounded by V_{576}, 3 HM_6 pass through S_5 (the latter not appearing in V_{72}). Then the sum of dihedral angles is 360°. So this is a space filling.

Reduced R_4 polygon.

§ 55. We will introduce again the *reduced* R_4 polygon of the 7-dimensional polytopes and the *reduced* R_4 polyhedron of the 8-dimensional ones. The former does not differ from the R_4 polygon in the case of S_7 and Cr_7. The following list contains the reduced R_4 polygons, the lengths of the edges of the space polyhedron passing through their vertices and the dihedral angles (between bounding R_5) which correspond to the plane angles of the polygon.

S_7	$(1, 1, 1)$	(α, α, α)
Cr_7	$(1, 1, 1, 1)$	$(\beta, \beta, \beta, \beta)$
V_{56}	$(1, 1, 1)$	(γ, δ, δ)
V_{126}	$(\sqrt{2}, \sqrt{2}, \sqrt{2})$	$(\varepsilon, \varepsilon, \varepsilon)$
	$(\sqrt{2}, 1, 1)$	$(\varepsilon, \eta, \eta)$

One kind of bounding polytope.

§ 56. We cannot bound a polytope by means of one kind of polytope.

The cases S_7 and Cr_7 are excluded for the same reason as S_6 and Cr_6 in the preceding discussion (art. 49)

In the case of V_{56} the dihedral angles are 120° and more.

In the case of V_{126} the vertices of the R_4 polyhedron are 3-angular. Hence that polyhedron is a tetrahedron, and it is impossible to construct a tetrahedron by means of the corresponding R_4 triangles.

Two kinds of bouding polytopes.

§ 57. We cannot combine V_{56} with any other. It is represented in the R_8 polytope by P_8. Now the adjacent polyhedra at the squares are necessarily other P_8. This must be rejected, the dihedral angle at a lateral edge corresponding to 120°.

We can combine V_{126} with other polytopes. Let us consider triangle $(\sqrt{2}, \sqrt{2}, \sqrt{2})$. The adjacent faces are necessarily of the same kind. So we get a tetrahedron bounded by four $(\sqrt{2}, \sqrt{2}, \sqrt{2})$. The other triangle which corresponds to V_{126} is $(\sqrt{2}, 1, 1)$. The adjacent faces at the edges $(\sqrt{2}, 1)$ are triangles of the same kind. So the fourth face is necessarily the $(1, 1, 1)$ corresponding to S_7. The sum of angles is 3ε and $\eta + 2\alpha$, both $< 360°$. So we can admit two kinds of reduced R_4 polyhedra. Let us now consider the corresponding original R_4 polyhedra. We find for that which corresponds to the former kind T, and for the latter kind a 3-angular pyramid whose base is limited by edges 1, and whose lateral edges are $\sqrt{2}$.

Now, the R_3 polytope which answers these conditions is a pyramid whose base is T and whose lateral edges are $\sqrt{2}$. This polytope is bounded by 1 polyhedron of the former and by 4 of the latter kind, and may be represented by

$$(1 + 4,\ 4 + 6,\ 4 + 6,\ 1 + 4).$$

Let x be the number of the vertices of the R_2 polytope; then the number of its limits are

$$x,\ \frac{x}{2} + 2x,\ x\,p_4 + 2x\,p_3,\ x\,\mathrm{T} + x\,\mathrm{P}_3,\ \frac{x}{5}\,\mathrm{C}_5 + \frac{x}{2}\,\mathrm{P}_\mathrm{T}$$

whence, by EULER'S theorem,

$$x = 10$$

This polytope is $\mathrm{P}_{\mathrm{C}_5}$, a prism whose bases are C_5, $(10, 5+20, 10p_4 + 20p_3,\ 10\mathrm{T} + 10\mathrm{P}_3,\ 2\mathrm{C}_5 + 5\mathrm{P}_\mathrm{T})$. Let y and z represent the number of vertices of the R_1 polytope and the R_0 polytope respectively, then we find for the number of their limits

$$y,\ 5y,\ \left(\frac{5}{3} + \frac{20}{3}\right)y,\ \left(\frac{5}{3} + 5\right)y,\ (2+1)y,\ \left(\frac{1}{3} + \frac{1}{3}\right)y;$$

$$z, \frac{yz}{2}, \frac{5yz}{3}, \left(\frac{5}{12}+\frac{5}{3}\right)yz, \left(\frac{5}{24}+1\right)yz,$$

$$\left(\frac{1}{3}+\frac{1}{16}\right)yz, \left(\frac{1}{21}+\frac{1}{96}\right)yz,$$

whence, by EULER'S theorem,

$$z\left(1-\frac{31}{672}y\right)=2.$$

Now $$1<\frac{31}{672}y,$$

whence $$y<22.$$

Besides the latter polytope is bounded i. a. by HM_6. Hence $z>32$ and thus $y>20$. So $y=21$. So the limits of the R_1 polytope and R_0 polytope are

$$64, 672, 2240, (560+2240)T, 1344\ S_4+280Cr_4,$$
$$448\ S_5+84HM_5, 64\ S_6+14HM_6.$$

This is HM_7.

Finally we can combine S_7 and Cr_7. Just as in art. 43 we must consider the R_4 polyhedron P_3. This leads to the R_0 polytope V_{56}. So we have to consider the following cases:

A. HM_7 is vertex polytope.

B. V_{56} is vertex polytope.

(2160, 69120, 483840, 1209600 1209600, 544320, 144960, 17520.) § 58. Case **A**. HM_7 is vertex polytope.

The circumradius of HM_7 being $\frac{1}{4}\sqrt{14}$, that of the polytope is $\sqrt{2}$.

Hence one of its vertices is represented by

$$0, 0, 0, 0, 0, 0, 0, 4a, \quad . \quad . \quad . \quad (1) \qquad \left(a=\frac{1}{4}\sqrt{2}\right)$$

and the corresponding vertex polytope by

$$\}a, a, a, a, a, a, a\{, 3a \quad . \quad . \quad . \quad . \quad . \quad (2)$$

Let us determine the vertex polytope of vertex

$$a, a, a, a, a, a, a, 3a$$

of (2). Its centre is

$$\tfrac{3}{4}a,\ \tfrac{3}{4}a,\ \tfrac{3}{4}a,\ \tfrac{3}{4}a,\ \tfrac{3}{4}a,\ \tfrac{3}{4}a,\ \tfrac{3}{4}a,\ \tfrac{9}{4}a.$$

To its vertices belong (1) and those 21 derived from (2) by changing two signs of a. Those 6 among the latter whose first coordinate have the sign — limit in connection with (1) a S_7. Opposite to its centre is situated a vertex of HM_7:

$$3a,\ a,\ a,\ a,\ a,\ a,\ a,\ a.$$

In this way we get 7 new vertices by placing $3a$ at either of the first 7 places.

In order to find the 35 remaining vertices of HM_7 we determine the 7 vertices opposite to the 7 new vertices in the M_7 from which the present HM_7 is derived. They are cointained in

$$-\tfrac{3}{2}a,\ \tfrac{1}{2}a,\ \tfrac{1}{2}a,\ \tfrac{1}{2}a,\ \tfrac{1}{2}a,\ \tfrac{1}{2}a,\ \tfrac{1}{2}a,\ \tfrac{7}{2}a,\ \ldots \quad (3)$$

with $-\tfrac{3}{2}a$ on either of the first 7 places. Now, if we choose 6 from them e. g. those which have $-\tfrac{3}{2}a$ on the 6 first places, then we are able to determine, with the help of (1), the centre of a M_6 which bounds M_7, i. e.

$$\tfrac{1}{2}a,\ \tfrac{1}{2}a,\ \tfrac{1}{2}a,\ \tfrac{1}{2}a,\ \tfrac{1}{2}a,\ \tfrac{1}{2}a,\ \tfrac{3}{2}a,\ \tfrac{5}{2}a.$$

This is the centre of a HM_6 which bounds the vertex polytope. Those 15 vertices whose first coordinate has the sign + belong to its vertices. Now, the vertices of HM_6 being situated symmetrically with respect to the centre we get as new vertices those derived from

$$2a,\ 2a,\ 0,\ 0,\ 0,\ 0,\ 2a,\ 2a$$

by the permutations of $2a$, $2a$ on the 6 first places. By chosing other sets of 6 vertices from (3) we find 35 vertices which complete the vertex polytope and which are contained in

$$(2a,\ 2a,\ 2a,\ 0,\ 0,\ 0,\ 0),\ 2a \quad \ldots \quad (4)$$

Now, by determining the vertex polytope corresponding to all the vertices (2) we get the following new vertices

$[2a,\ 2a,\ 2a,\ 0,\ 0,\ 0,\ 0],\ a$. (5), number = 280

$\{3a,\ a,\ a,\ a,\ a,\ a,\ a\},\ a$. (6), „ = 448

We will determine the vertex polytope corresponding to one of the vertices (5), i. e. to

$$2a, 2a, 2a, 0, 0, 0, 0, 2a.$$

Of its vertices 8 are contained in (2), 24 in (5) and 24 in (6). The 8 remaining are the vertices of a Cr_4:

$$2a, 2a, 2a, [2a, 0, 0, 0], 0.$$

So we get 560 new vertices

$$[2a, 2a, 2a, 2a, 0, 0, 0], 0 \quad . \quad . \quad . \quad . \quad (7)$$

If we determine the vertex polytope to one of the vertices (6), e. g. to

$$3a, a, a, a, a, a, a, a,$$

it appears that 63 vertices have been determined already viz. 1 of (2), 15 of (5), 27 of (6) and 20 of (7). The missing one is

$$4a, 0, 0, 0, 0, 0, 0, 0.$$

Hence we get 14 new vertices

$$[4a, 0, 0, 0, 0, 0, 0], 0 \quad . \quad . \quad . \quad . \quad . \quad (8)$$

We infer from the symbols (7) and (8) that the vertices are situated symmetrically with respect to the centre. Hence the number of vertices is 2160. We can represent them by

$$\begin{array}{ll} [4a, 0, 0, 0, 0, 0, 0, 0], \text{ number} & = 16 \\ \{3a, a, a, a, a, a, a, a\}, \quad " & = 1024 \\ [2a, 2a, 2a, 2a, 0, 0, 0, 0], \quad " & = 1120 \\ \hline & 2160. \end{array}$$

Its limits are

$$2160,\ 69120,\ 483840\, p_3,\ 1209600\, T,\ (241920 + 967680)\, C_5,$$
$$483840\, S_5 + 60480\, Cr_5,\ 138240\, S_6 + 6720\, V_{27},$$
$$17280\, S_7 + 240\, V_{126}.$$

Its degree of regularity is $\dfrac{4\frac{1}{2}}{8} = \dfrac{9}{16}$.

(240, 6720, 60480, 241920, 483840, 483840, 207360, 19440) § 59. Case **B.** V_{56} is vertex polytope.

The circumradius is 1, that of V_{56} being $\frac{1}{2}\sqrt{3}$.

Hence we can represent one vertex by

$$0, 0, 0, 0, 0, 0, 0, 1$$

and the vertices of the corresponding vertex polytope (art. 50) by

$$\begin{array}{llllll} 0, 0, 0, 0, & 0, & 0, & 3c, & \frac{1}{2} \\ 0, 0, 0, 0, & 0, & 4b, & c, & \frac{1}{2} \\ \{a, a, a, a, & a\}, & b, & c, & \frac{1}{2} \\ [2a, 0, 0, 0, & 0], & -2b, & c, & \frac{1}{2} \\ [2a, 0, 0, 0, & 0], & 2b, & -c, & \frac{1}{2} \\ \{-a, a, a, a, & a\}, & -b, & -c, & \frac{1}{2} \\ 0, 0, 0, 0, & 0, & -4b, & -c, & \frac{1}{2} \\ 0, 0, 0, 0, & 0, & 0, & -3c, & \frac{1}{2} \end{array}$$

It is easy to determine the vertex polytopes corresponding to these vertices, the vertices of V_{56} being situated symmetrically with respect to the centre. The following list contains those whose eighth coordinate is 0.

$$\begin{array}{lllll} 0, & 0, 0, 0, 0, & \{4b, -2c\}, 0, & \text{number} = & 2 \\ \{a, & a, a, a, a\}, & \{b, -2c\}, 0, & \text{,,} \quad = & 32 \\ [2a, & 0, 0, 0, 0], & \{2b, \ 2c\}, 0, & \text{,,} \quad = & 20 \\ [2a, & 2a, 0, 0, 0], & 0, \quad 0, 0, & \text{,,} \quad = & 32 \\ \hline & & & & 126. \end{array}$$

It appears from these symbols that the vertices of the present polytope are symmetrical with respect to its centre. Hence their number is: $126 + 2 . 57 = 240$.

We can transform the coordinates so as to represent the vertices by two symbols:

$$\begin{array}{ll} \{a, a, a, a, a, a, a, a\}, & \text{number} = 128 \\ [2a, 2a, 0, 0, 0, 0, 0, 0], & \text{,,} \quad = 112 \\ \hline & 240. \end{array}$$

Its symbol of characteristic numbers is:

$$240, 6720, 60480, 241920, 483840, 483840,$$
$$(69120 + 138240) S_6, \ 17280 S_7 + 2160 Cr_7.$$

Its degree of regularity is $\frac{6\frac{1}{2}}{8} = \frac{13}{16}$.

Conclusion. § 60. We will now demonstrate that there are no other semiregular polytopes. The following list contains the dihedral angles at a bounding R_6 of S_8, Cr_8 and the polytopes of art. 58 and 59, the latter represented by V_{2160} and V_{240} respectively.

	Dihedral angles
S_8	$82^\circ\,49'\,10'' = \alpha$
Cr_8	$138^\circ\,35'\,26'' = \beta$
V_{2160}	$(V_{126}, V_{126}) = 120^\circ = \varepsilon$
	$(S_7, V_{126}) = 138^\circ\,35'\,25'' = \eta$
V_{240}	$(Cr_7, Cr_7) = \eta$
	$(S_7, Cr_7) = 152^\circ\,6'\,52'' = \delta$

We cannot bound a polytope by S_8 only, for the reason given in art. 43, nor by Cr_8, V_{2160} or V_{240} only, the angles being 120° or more.

We can try to combine S_8 with an other polytope. The combination of S_8 and Cr_8 would lead (compare page 123) to the vertex polytope V_{240}. This must be rejected, its circumradius being $= 1$.

The combination of S_8 and V_{240} must be rejected, 3 Cr_7 and consequently 3 angles η meeting at a bounding S_6. For the same reason the combinations of S_8 with V_{2160}, of Cr_8 with V_{240}, and of Cr_8 with V_{2160} lead to no result.

Finally we cannot construct a polytope bounded by V_{240} and V_{2160}. The adjacent polytope of V_{2160} is necessarily another V_{2160}, V_{126} not appearing in V_{240}. This leads to a space filling.

On the next page we enumerate the resulting polytopes with a regularity $\frac{1}{2}$ or more.

SUMMARY OF THE POLYTOPES OF THE FIRST KIND.

Notation	R_0	R_1	R_2	R_3	R_4	R_5	R_6	R_7	page
tC_5	10	30	$(10+20)p_3$	$5O+5T$					14
tC_8	32	96	$64p_3+24p_4$	$8CO+16T$					16
tC_{24}	96	288	$96p_3+144p_4$	$24CO+24C$					18
tC_{600}	720	3600	$(1200+2400)p_3$	$600O+120I$					22
tC_{120}	1200	3600	$2400p_3+720p_5$	$120ID+600T$					29
	30	60	$20p_3+20p_6$	$10tT$					41
	288	576	$192p_3+144p_8$	$48tC$					46
	20	60	$40p_3+30p_4$	$10T+20P_3$					51
	144	576	$384p_3+288p_4$	$48O+192P_3$					53
	n^2	$2n^2$	$n^2p_4+2np_n$	$2nP_n$					57
S_5^2	20	90	$120p_3$	$30T+30O$	$12tC_5$				79
HM_5	16	80	$160p_3$	$(80+40)T$	$16C_5+10C_{16}$				82
S_5^1	15	60	$(20+60)p_3$	$30T+15O$	$6C_5+6tC_5$				86
Cr_5^1	40	240	$(80+320)p_3$	$160T+80O$	$32tC_5+10C_{16}$				89
Cr_5^2	80	480	$(320+320)p_3$	$80T+200O$	$32tC_5+10C_{24}$				92
V_{72}	72	720	$2160p_3$	$2160T$	$432C_5+270C_{16}$	$54HM_5$			104
HM_6	32	240	$640p_3$	$(160+480)T$	$192C_5+60C_{16}$	$32S_5+12HM_5$			108
V_{27}	27	216	$720p_3$	$1080T$	$216C_5+432C_5$	$72S_5+27Cr_5$			109
V_{56}	56	756	$4032p_3$	$10080T$	$12096C_5$	$(2016+4032)S_5$	$576S_6+126Cr_6$		116
V_{126}	126	2016	$10080p_3$	$20160T$	$(4032+12096)C_5$	$4032S_5+756Cr_5$	$576S_6+56V_{27}$		117
V_{576}	576	10080	$40320p_3$	$(30240+20160)T$	$16128C_5+7560C_{16}$	$2016S_5+2268HM_5$	$126HM_6+56V_{72}$		118
V_{2160}	2160	69120	$483840p_3$	$1209600T$	$(241920+967680)C_5$	$483840S_5+60480Cr_5$	$138240S_6+6720V_{27}$	$17280S_7+240V_{126}$	123
V_{240}	240	6720	$60480p_3$	$241920T$	$483840C_5$	$483840S_5$	$(69120+138240)S_6$	$17280S_7+2160Cr_7$	125

APPENDIX.

ON THE CONNECTION OF THE DEGREE OF REGULARITY OF A POLYTOPE AND THAT OF ITS VERTEX POLYTOPE.

In several arts. of the present essay the degree of regularity of a polytope has been mentioned without a detailed consideration of its characteristics of regularity. In those cases we derived it from the degree of regularity of its vertex polytope, if the latter had been described in the preceding chapter. Indeed, by the very fact that a polytope admits a vertex polytope, its vertices are equal. Moreover, equal vertices of the vertex polytope correspond to equal edges of the polytope, equal edges of the former correspond to equal faces of the latter, etc. Hence it is obvious that *the number of characteristics of the polytope is one more than that of its vertex polytope.*

For instance, the polytope of § 59 shows $6\frac{1}{2}$, that of § 50 shows $5\frac{1}{2}$ characteristics; those of § 51 en § 45 show $4\frac{1}{2}$ and $3\frac{1}{2}$ respectively.

An *exception* must be made for the case where the *vertex polytope* has *no characteristics.* Then the polytope has $1\frac{1}{2}$ *characteristics.* Indeed the polytope has 1 characteristic as soon as it admits a vertex polytope and moreover $\frac{1}{2}$ characteristic, its vertices being at equal distances from those of the vertex polytope.

An instance is tT, with $1\frac{1}{2}$ characteristic; its vertex polytope is an isosceles triangle with no characteristic.

An other instance may be found page 122, where a space polytope is described $(1+4,\ 4+6,\ 4+6,\ 1+4)$ without characteristic. The corresponding face polytope (i. e. the polytope to which the former corresponds as vertex polytope) has $1\frac{1}{2}$ characteristics, the edge polytope $2\frac{1}{2}$, the vertex polytope $3\frac{1}{2}$ and the polytope itself (§ 58) $4\frac{1}{2}$ characteristics.

So we can state the following

Rule. *If the degree of regularity of a vertex polytope is* $\frac{p}{n}$, *then that of the polytope is* $\frac{p+1}{n+1}$. *The case where* $p=0$ *makes exception. Then the degree of regularity is* $\frac{1\frac{1}{2}}{n+1}$.

The same rule holds for a space filling which shows some characteristics of regularity.

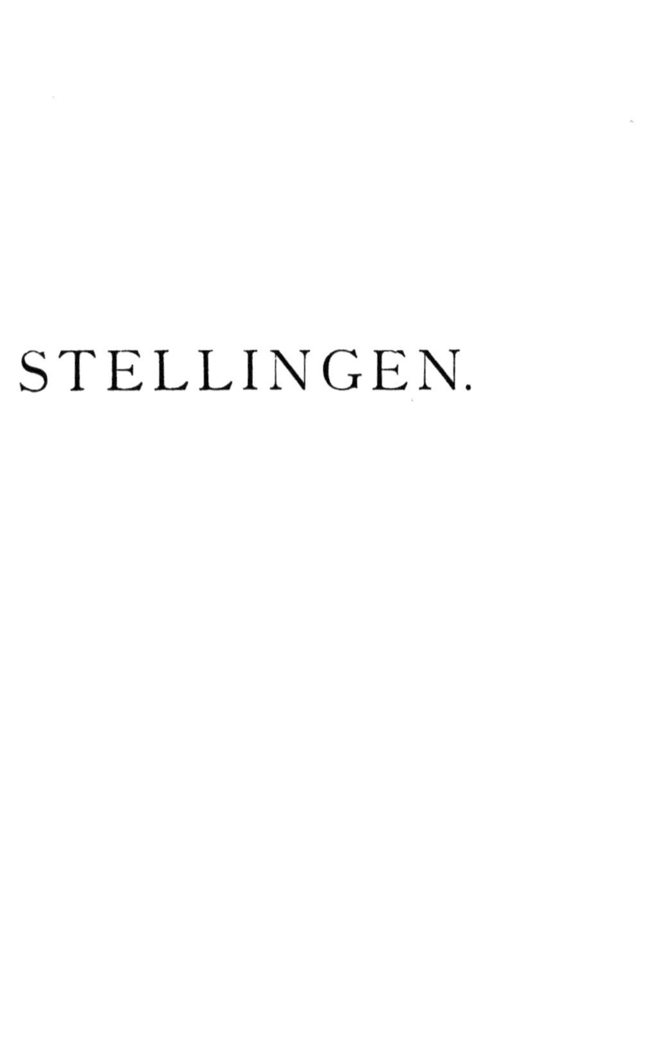

STELLINGEN.

STELLINGEN.

I.

Met behulp van de methode van Mrs. A. BOOLE STOTT zijn de polytopen der hoofdstukken V, VI en VII van dit proefschrift waarschijnlijk niet af te leiden.

(Mrs. A. BOOLE STOTT, Geometrical deduction of semiregular from regular polytopes and space fillings, Verh. Kon. Akad. Amsterdam, 1e sectie, XI, No. 1).

II.

Er is voor het gebruik der notatie „R_{-1}" voor de doorsnede van twee onafhankelijke ruimten nog een andere rechtvaardiging te geven dan die voorkomende in het leerboek van Dr. P. H. SCHOUTE.

(Dr. P. H. SCHOUTE, Mehrdimensionale Geometrie, I, pag. 14).

III.

Door beschouwing van het maatpolytoop komt Dr. ANTON PUCHTA tot het volgende theorema:

„In der allgemeinen Gruppe von $2n$ Elementen ist eine ausgezeichnete Untergruppe enthalten, welche die Ordnung hat: $n!\,2^{n-1}$."

Dit theorema is onjuist.

(Sitzungsberichte Akad. d. Wiss. Wien, Math. Naturw. Classe, **89**, II, pag. 837).

IV.

Dr. ANTON PUCHTA leidt nog dit theorema af:

„In der Gruppe P von der Ordnung $n!\,2^{n-1}$ der $2n$ Elemente T_{n-1} ist eine weitere ausgezeichnete Untergruppe Q von der Ordnung $n!\,2^{n-2}$ enthalten."

De schrijver beweert nu, dat voor $n = 4$ de ondergroep Q de groep der rotaties van het kruispolytoop is. Dit is onjuist.

(Zelfde verhandeling, pag. 840).

V.

Gewoonlijk vindt men in de leerboeken der levensverzekeringswiskunde voor het aantal vrouwen, die uit een groep van $l_x\, l_y$ (y-jarige met x-jarige mannen gehuwde) vrouwen, in de loop van één jaar weduwe worden:

$$l_x\, l_y\, q_x (1 - q_y).$$

Beter is:

$$l_x\, l_y\, q_x (1 - \tfrac{1}{2} q_y).$$

(Zie o. a. Corneille L. Landré, Dr. August Zillmer, Dr. W. Grossmann).

VI.

De Geometrographie van LEMOINE heeft veel kunstmatigs.

VII.

De eigenschap bekend als *Gibbs' paradox*, dat de toename der entropie bij menging van twee gassen onafhankelijk is van den aard dier gassen, behoeft geen aanleiding te geven tot ongerijmde gevolgtrekkingen.

VIII.

MAXWELL's bewering, dat de theorie der magnetische inductie kan worden afgeleid "without any assumptions except those of the dynamical theory as stated in Chapter VII", is niet juist.

(JAMES CLERK MAXWELL, A Treatise on Electricity and Magnetism, 1892, II, page 229).

IX.

In verband met de wet van DULONG en PETIT zegt KUENEN: „De moleculaire theorieën betreffende den vasten toestand zijn echter vooralsnog niet ver genoeg gevorderd, om de beteekenis van deze wet, die ontwijfelbaar althans bij benadering juist is, en van de uitzonderingen volledig in te zien."

RICHARZ heeft echter langs kinetischen weg een vrij bevredigende verklaring der wet gegeven.

(F. RICHARZ, Ueber das Gesetz von Dulong und Petit, Wied. Ann., N. F., **48**, 708.

BOSSCHA—KUENEN, Leerboek der Natuurkunde, 1899, 2e boek, pag. 308).

X.

In het leerboek der natuurkunde van dr. G. C. GERRITS wordt de eenheid in de behandeling der lenzen onnoodig verbroken.

XI.

Het is ongewenscht practische oefeningen in de natuurkunde in te voeren aan de hoogere burgerscholen met vijfjarigen cursus.

XII.

Grondige hervorming van het wiskundeonderwijs aan de hoogere burgerscholen is zeer noodzakelijk.

www.ingramcontent.com/pod-product-compliance
Lightning Source LLC
LaVergne TN
LVHW010610110826
845149LV00003B/852

* 9 7 8 1 4 1 8 1 7 9 6 8 7 *